ACTIVITIES ON BLACKLINE MASTERS FOR BEGINNING WRITERS OF ENGLISH

CLAUDIA J. RUCINSKI

Lifelong Learning Books
SCOTT, FORESMAN AND COMPANY
Glenview, Illinois • London, England

To my parents, Edmund and Delphine Rucinski,
for instilling in me a love of language and an
appreciation for the grace and beauty of other cultures.

Copyright © 1990 Claudia J. Rucinski.
All Rights Reserved.
Printed in the United States of America.

The user of this work is granted permission to photocopy individual pages for classroom use only.

This book is protected by Copyright and permission should be obtained from the publisher prior to any prohibited reproduction, storage in a retrieval system, or transmission in any other form or by any other means, electronic, mechanical, or otherwise. For information regarding permission, write to Scott, Foresman and Company, 1900 East Lake Avenue, Glenview, Illinois 60025.

D'Nealian® Handwriting is a registered trademark of Donald N. Thurber, licensed exclusively by Scott, Foresman and Company, and is used here with permission.

ISBN 0-673-24575-6

23456 EBI 9594939291

Acknowledgments

I would like to thank the following people for their support of this project: Thomas, Marcia, and Meghan Marciniak; Somvang Phromkharanourak; my colleagues at The Milwaukee Area Technical College, especially Donna Bartolone, Rosemary Chavez, JoEllen Christians, Mark Mankowski, Beverly Mioskowski, Joyce Nicolazzi, and Susan Snyder; Joan Wotta; and Linda Rousos, currently teaching at Pima Community College in Arizona. I am also greatly indebted to my colleague, Cheryl Kirchner, for her valuable assistance, and to Christine Bunn.

 I extend this appreciation as well to my editor, Roseanne Mendoza, for her constant support and encouragement and to Elaine Goldberg for her final careful editing of the manuscript.

 And to my father, Edmund J. Rucinski, I would like to extend a special note of thanks for his gift of drawings. Without his insight, ideas, and talent this book would never have been possible.

 Finally, I would like to thank the extraordinary group of people who have been my students. I am at a loss as to how to repay them for all they have taught me.

Contents

Acknowledgments *ii*
About *Cuing In*
    Organization and Format *iv*
    Placement of Students *vi*

LESSON 1   Visual Discrimination (Masters 1–13) *1*
LESSON 2   The Alphabet (Masters 14–62) *3*
LESSON 3   Name (Masters 63–73) *7*
LESSON 4   Numbers 1–10 (Masters 74–90) *12*
LESSON 5   Telephone Number (Masters 91–93) *14*
LESSON 6   Social Security Number (Masters 94–96) *16*
CHECKUP 1   (Master 97) *17*
LESSON 7   Numbers 11–19 (Masters 98–109) *18*
LESSON 8   Numbers 20–100 (Masters 110–120) *21*
LESSON 9   Address-Number and Street
    (Masters 121–128) *24*
WORD SEARCH 1   (Master 129) *27*
LESSON 10   Address-City, State, and Zip Code
    (Masters 130–136) *28*
WORD SEARCH 2   (Master 137) *31*
CHECKUP 2   (Master 138) *31*
LESSON 11   Marital Status (Masters 139–143) *32*
LESSON 12   Sex (Masters 144–146) *34*
LESSON 13   Formal Titles (Masters 147–148) *36*
CHECKUP 3   (Master 149) *37*
WORD SEARCH 3   (Master 150) *38*
LESSON 14   Height and Weight (Masters 151–156) *39*
LESSON 15   Color of Hair and Eyes
    (Masters 157–160) *42*
WORD SEARCH 4   (Master 161) *44*
LESSON 16   Place of Birth (Masters 162–164) *45*
LESSON 17   Age (Masters 165–166) *48*
LESSON 18   Date (Masters 167–189) *50*
CHECKUPS 4–8   (Masters 190–194) *52*
BLACKLINE MASTERS   1–194
STUDENT PROGRESS CHART   (Follows Master 194)

About *Cuing In*

Cuing In contains reading and writing activities designed to aid adult learners of English as a Second Language (ESL) in attaining literacy in English. It may be used as an independent text, as a prelude to *Write on Cue,* or in conjunction with *Write on Cue. Cuing In* is suitable for use in a whole group setting, in a multilevel classroom, or in one-on-one tutoring.

Cuing In is appropriate for use as a first reading and writing text for students who are unfamiliar with the English language. The background and levels of these students will vary. Some of them may be at a level of preliteracy; that is, they are not literate in their own language and do not understand the concept that oral speech may be represented in written form. Other students may be illiterate in their own language as well as in English but have some understanding of the written word representing the spoken word but, perhaps for lack of opportunity for formal education in their home country, have not attained literacy. For both these groups of students, simply holding a pencil may be uncomfortable. Other students may be literate in their own language, but that language may use a non-Roman alphabet. These students must learn to identify and form the letters in the Roman alphabet.

Many of these students lack oral skills in English as well. Some students at the very beginner level will be unable to respond to the question, What's your name? Other students —while able to say their name, address, and telephone number—will be unable to write this information or read the words *name, address,* and *telephone number. Cuing In* intends to serve the needs of all the above groups of students.

For those students who lack literacy and also are unable to respond to basic questions such as, What is your name? the development of oral skills should be stressed first. After sufficient oral work, the development of literacy skills can then follow.

Literacy is necessary to truly function in our society, and in this sense *Cuing In* is a functional text. You may wish to combine the literacy units presented here with other units in the ESL curriculum for beginners. For example, Lessons 4, 7, and 8 focus on the numbers 1–100. These lessons may be combined with a unit on money.

ORGANIZATION AND FORMAT OF *CUING IN*

Cuing In is not a student workbook but rather a series of lessons presented on blackline masters that may be photocopied. There are two advantages to this system. One is that you may distribute the copies to suit the needs of the students. If a student has difficulty in a particular area, you, after tutoring that student, may redistribute the appropriate handouts. In this way, the student does not feel the embarrassment of having to erase and do the lesson again.

Another advantage is that you can control the distribution of the handouts so that students will not proceed too quickly. Some diligent and motivated students will keep working in their workbooks even though they may not fully understand a lesson. This may contribute to errors that later have to be corrected. Such corrections may be a demoralizing experience for the students and may hinder further progress.

The masters may also be used to make transparencies for an overhead projector. This use of transparencies may prove particularly beneficial when working with a group of students.

Because students will have many individual papers, it is suggested that they purchase a three-ring binder or a clip folder to hold the handouts. This will organize the lessons and produce a real "book" for students. The accumulation and organization of these handouts may also contribute to a sense of accomplishment.

Cuing In is arranged in eighteen lessons, each focusing on a specific area. Checkups on previously learned material are provided after every few lessons. In addition, there are several Word Search activities for students that provide word-recognition practice and entertainment at the same time. Each lesson includes the following:

1. *Objectives.* The objectives of the lesson are stated to define its focus.
2. *Materials Needed.* The handouts needed as well as extra materials for the completion of the activities are listed.
3. *New Vocabulary.* The new words that are focused on in the lesson are listed. These are the words that are most important to the student as he or she works through the lesson.
4. *Sequence of Activities.* Instructions are given as to the order of distribution of the handouts as well as suggestions for the use of oral activities. Lessons are organized around Review, Introduction of Concept, Reading and Writing Practice, and Follow-up.
5. *Notes.* Because no one can foresee all possible problems a student may encounter while studying a lesson, notes are presented that may alert you to possible obstacles in a student's progress. Obviously not all of these potential problems may be addressed, but the Notes may help you become aware of potential problems before these create greater difficulties for the student.

Most lessons are organized as follows:

1. *Review.* Activities that serve as a warm-up for the new material in the lesson are suggested. Emphasis is on oral practice. No handout is involved in this part of the lesson.
2. *Introduction of Concept.* The concept of the lesson is presented in a visual manner on a handout. In most cases, no words appear on the handout so students are not burdened with the written word while they are trying to understand the concept.
3. *Reading and Writing Practice.* Instructions are included for the distribution and completion of handouts that foster abilities in reading and writing.

Students have the opportunity to practice recognizing the vocabulary before being expected to actually use it. After completion of these handouts, students are able to read and write the information that was previously seen.

Because students learn at their own pace, it cannot be assumed that all students will learn the lesson in one class session. Many of the lessons will require several class sessions for all students. Some students may have to do the exercises several times, but care should be taken to prevent a student from becoming frustrated or bored. You may want to consider having a student *complete* the exercises for homework, thus relieving him or her of having to perform correctly in class. Completing the exercises at home may be more relaxed for the student, and for many students homework carries with it a certain status. When the student brings in the completed homework, review it with him or her. But exercise caution with regard to homework: only assign homework to students after they have already done part of the exercise in class under guidance. Homework should represent extra practice for work that has already been attempted in class.

4. *Follow-up.* Suggestions for oral activities that incorporate the concepts of the lesson are given. No handouts are used in this part of the lesson.

It's Your Cue. In the final section of many lessons, students apply the knowledge they have learned.

The exercises parallel those of *Write on Cue.* In this way, then, the student will already possess the skills necessary to complete the exercises in *Write on Cue.* Lessons in *Cuing In* focus on personal information.

Cuing In has a structured format because often students at this level respond well to consistency. Students seem to welcome this systematic presentation; it gives them security by allowing them the opportunity to build their confidence. By proceeding in a step-by-step manner, students increase their chances for success. Students, for example, may feel a sense of accomplishment after understanding that they are to circle the word that is the same as another word or match two words. This may not seem important to people who have had the benefit of formal education, but students who have not had this benefit may feel a true sense of achievement. This positive attitude plays a crucial role in their further development of literacy.

The consistent format of the lessons could be viewed as unexciting, but when the activities are presented by a skilled instructor, the lesson can be fun! To simply hand out the exercises to students without oral preparation or oral follow-up would be inconsistent with the design of the activities and their ultimate purpose.

As many ESL instructors know, students at the beginner level may lack literacy and oral proficiency in English, but they have much to offer. Their motivation and diligence fill an instructor with admiration and respect. Many of these students have come through times of great difficulty and now are acutely aware of what they lack for survival in a new society. *Cuing In* provides these students with a vehicle for the attainment of literacy, which is a skill necessary for their survival. Perhaps by easing their transition to literacy, students may feel some encouragement for their future.

The activities in *Cuing In* were born of the author's experience with her students, who found the activities beneficial and fun. It is hoped that they may prove the same for you and your students.

PLACEMENT OF STUDENTS

It may not be necessary for every student to begin with Lesson 1. To determine a student's placement, consider the following:

1. Student's educational background. Examine the student's educational background, including the years of education in the native country as well as the educational experience in the United States.

2. Student's literacy. Determine the student's literacy. Is the student literate in the native language? What alphabet is used in the native language? Attaining literacy in English may be different for the student whose native language uses the Roman alphabet as opposed to one whose alphabet is distinctly different from the Roman alphabet. There is not always a link between oral ability and literacy. Some students may speak three languages but be illiterate in all three.

3. Results of a placement test. Use the Checkups provided after certain lessons as placement tests. For example, the student may begin by using the first Checkup as a placement measure. If students are unable to respond correctly to all items, they should be given handout 1. If students are able to respond correctly, they may be given the next Checkup, and so on, until they are unable to complete an exercise successfully.

LESSON 1 | Visual Discrimination

OBJECTIVE To distinguish between shapes that are similar but not the same.

MATERIALS NEEDED handouts from blackline masters 1–13

NEW VOCABULARY same
different

INTRODUCTION OF CONCEPT

Discuss the concepts of "same" and "different." This may be done by pointing to various objects in the classroom, in pictures, and so on. Ask students to identify items as being the "same" or "different." (This is to prepare the students for distinguishing letters, which is a necessary skill for reading.)

READING AND WRITING PRACTICE

1. Draw shapes on the board and use them to show "same" or "different." Distribute handouts 1 and 2. Tell students to look at all the shapes in each row, find the one that is different, and then draw a circle around it. Go over the first examples with students. If they seem to understand the directions, instruct them to continue with the rest of the rows of shapes. While students are working individually, go around the room to see that they have understood the directions and are proceeding in the correct manner.

2. When students have correctly completed handouts 1 and 2, distribute handouts 3 and 4. Ask students to look at the first shape in each row and all the shapes beside it, find the shape that is the same as the first shape in the row, and draw a circle around that shape. Go over the example with students and then instruct them to continue.

3. Upon successful completion of handouts 3 and 4, distribute handouts 5 and 6. Read the direction to students and discuss it; then do the example with the whole group. As before, watch students as they complete the exercise to be certain that they understand how to do the task.

4. Distribute handouts 7–13, which represent another set of shapes, and proceed in the manner described in procedures 1, 2, and 3.

NOTES If a student has great difficulty with the discrimination exercises, he or she may have a physical problem. The student may need glasses, or the problem may be more serious. Many students have visual problems as a result of eye injuries received during war. It may be best to talk with the student or a family member concerning this.

Some students may not have a visual problem but may have difficulty following the directions. Other students may have problems understanding "same" and "different." Determining the cause of the problem may present a challenge.

LESSON 2 | The Alphabet

OBJECTIVES
1. To identify the letters of the alphabet orally.
2. To write the letters of the alphabet in both upper and lower case.
3. To sequence the letters of the alphabet.

MATERIALS NEEDED
handouts from blackline masters 14–62
alphabet flash cards[1]
pin-back plastic letters[2]
bulletin board
alphabet bingo game

NEW VOCABULARY
letter
alphabet
(names of letters of the alphabet)

INTRODUCTION OF CONCEPT—Uppercase Letters

1. Write the letters of the alphabet on the blackboard, using capital letters only. Point to each letter and say its name. Have students repeat the letter name as they look at the indicated letter. Do this several times until students seem readily able to identify the letters.

2. Point to the letters in random order and ask students to name each letter indicated.

3. For sequencing of letters, go around the room and have each student say a letter. For example, the first student says, "A," the next student, "B," the next, "C." Students can look at the letters on the board for clarification.

4. Distribute handout 14. Say a letter and ask students to put a finger on that letter. One student may take the role of teacher and ask other students to point to the letter he or she designates. Students may also do this exercise in pairs or in small groups.

READING AND WRITING PRACTICE—Uppercase Letters

1. Distribute handouts 15 and 16. Instruct students to look at the first letter in each row and all the letters beside it, find the same

---

[1] If you make your own flash cards, write the capital letters on one color of paper (for example, yellow) and the small letters on another (for example, blue).

[2] These may be purchased at office supply stores for fifteen to twenty dollars.

letter as the first one in the row, and circle that letter. Do the examples with students and then have them proceed on their own.

2. Have students use the pin-back letters (capitals only) in a dictation exercise. Say a letter and call on a student to choose the letter from the group of letters and pin it on the bulletin board. Again, students may take the role of teacher and do this exercise in pairs or small groups.

3. Distribute handout 17. Write the letter *A* on the board, showing the strokes in the correct order. Work with students individually as they first trace and then copy the letter. Continue similarly with the letter *B*. Proceed in the same manner with the remaining letters of the alphabet, introducing the letters in alphabetical order (handouts 18–29). Some students may already know how to write the letters but write them in a manner different from that presented in the lesson. For example, some students write *S* by beginning the stroke at the bottom of the letter instead of at the top. Their way of forming the letter may seem more difficult, and you may want to encourage students to try to form the letter the new way.

INTRODUCTION OF CONCEPT—Lowercase Letters

1. Distribute handout 30. Explain that *a* is the same as *A* but sometimes *A* is used and at other times *a* is used. Write *A* on the board and identify it as "capital A." Next to it write *a* and identify it as "small a." Repeat the procedure for the other letters of the alphabet.

2. Point to lowercase forms of the alphabet on the board and ask students to identify each letter. Indicate the letters first in alphabetical order and then point to the letters in random order.

3. Distribute handout 31. As with the capital letters, say a letter and ask students to put a finger on that letter. One student may take the role of teacher and ask other students to point to the letter he or she designates. Students may also do this exercise in pairs or in small groups.

4. Using the flash cards, play a card game. Put the flash cards in two piles, the yellow pile of capital letters in one and the blue pile of small letters in another. Put the letters facedown. A student takes one card from the top of the yellow pile (capital letters) and one card from the top of the blue pile (small letters). If the two letters match, the student has a pair. If the small letter does not match the capital, the student must put the small-letter card at the bottom of the pile. The next student picks a card from the capital-letter pile, and the game proceeds. The student with the most pairs at the end of the game wins.

    Another game can be played by putting both piles of cards together and asking a student, a pair of students, or a small group working together to "find capital E" or "find small m," and so on. To increase the difficulty of this game, you may wish to make a set of flash cards with both capital and small letters in the same color. In this way, students will not have the color (yellow for capital, blue for small) to clue them in. The above games may also be done with the pin-back letters.

READING AND WRITING PRACTICE—Lowercase Letters

Distribute handout 32. Write the letter *a* on the board, showing the strokes in the correct order. Work with students individually as they first trace and then copy the letter. Continue similarly with the letter *b* and then the remaining letters in alphabetical order using handouts 33–44.

READING AND WRITING PRACTICE—Uppercase and Lowercase Letters

1. Distribute handouts 45 and 46. Tell students to match the capital and small letters. Do several matches with them until it is apparent that they understand the directions.
2. Distribute handouts 47 and 48. Ask students to circle the capital letter in each row of letters. There is only one capital letter per row.
3. Distribute handouts 49 and 50. Instruct students to circle *all* the capital letters in each row. Point out that there may be more than one capital letter per row.
4. Distribute handouts 51 and 52. Instruct students to circle the small letter in each row of letters. There is only one small letter per row.
5. Distribute handouts 53 and 54. Tell students to circle *all* the small letters in each row. Again, alert them that there may be more than one small letter per row.

FOLLOW-UP

Review the sequencing of letters by saying "a" and then going around the room and having students, in turn, say the next letter of the alphabet. Write the alphabet on the board and discuss "before" and "after"— "What letter comes after *a?*" "What letter comes before *m?*" and so on. Students may take the role of teacher and ask the questions of other students.

READING AND WRITING PRACTICE—Uppercase and Lowercase Letters

1. Ask students to sequence the letters of the alphabet using pin-back letters. Put all the flash cards in a pile and ask students to sequence the flash cards.
2. Distribute handouts 55 and 56. Explain that in this exercise students are to think about the order of the letters as they appear in the alphabet. Explain "cross out" to students as shown in the examples. Then instruct them to cross out the letter in each row that does not belong. Do several examples with students until you determine that they understand the directions. This exercise uses only capital letters.
3. Distribute handouts 57 and 58. Repeat the steps given in procedure 2. This exercise uses small letters.
4. Distribute handouts 59 and 60. Repeat the steps given in procedure 2. In this exercise both small and capital letters are used.

5. Distribute handout 61. Have students write the missing letters to complete the alphabet, using capital letters and then small letters.

6. Distribute handout 62. Ask students to write the entire alphabet in capital letters and then in small letters.

FOLLOW-UP

1. Write the first names of students on the board, spelling each name aloud while writing it. Then ask students to write their own first names on the board, spelling each name while they write it. Students may then write the names of their classmates. For example, the student may ask, "What's your name? How do you spell it?" You may have to explain to students what *spell* means.

2. Ask students to "spell" their names using the pin-back letters or flash cards. Tell students that the first letter of the name must be a capital letter.

3. Play alphabet bingo! This is good for letter recognition, since it presents the letters in both oral and written forms.

NOTES

While doing exercises on the board, emphasize that reading and writing are done from left to right.

The distinction between capital and small letters may be explained to accommodate the needs and abilities of the students. This distinction should not present a problem for students already familiar with the Roman alphabet. However, students whose native alphabets are non-Roman or students who are not literate in their native language may find this distinction more difficult. The extent of explanation and drill of these forms will vary. This usage can be reinforced in other areas, such as with name and address.

Students whose languages use a non-Roman alphabet may wish to write their alphabet for other class members. Some students may volunteer to show this without even being asked, while others may be very pleased to do so when asked. This can be a good exercise for increasing self-esteem, since students see that others appreciate their language. You may wish to bring a book to class that shows different alphabets.

For fun, you and the students may wish to try to write some letters from a foreign alphabet. This can be an excellent sensitizing experience for all, and often students seem fascinated by the languages and backgrounds of their classmates. By having an opportunity to present their own language, students enjoy a chance to be the "expert" for a change. It seems that everyone may benefit.

LESSON 3 | Name

OBJECTIVES
1. To understand the concept of first, middle, and last names.
2. To read the words *name, first, last,* and *middle* and supply the appropriate information in written and oral forms.

MATERIALS NEEDED
handouts from blackline masters 63–71, 72–73 (optional)
colored chalk
large sheets of colored paper

NEW VOCABULARY
name   last
first   middle

REVIEW

While pointing to a student, say the student's name. Do this for all students. Point to yourself and say your name. Then ask students individually, "What is your name?" After doing this several times, point to a student and ask the other students, "What's her name?" or "What's his name?"

INTRODUCTION OF CONCEPT

Distribute handout 63. Use the pictures on the handout to help explain first name, middle name, and last name.

READING AND WRITING PRACTICE

1. Using colored chalk, write the words *First, Middle,* and *Last* as three headings on the blackboard. Write each word in a different color—for example, *First* in blue, *Middle* in yellow, and *Last* in purple.

2. Write each student's names in the appropriate columns, using the same color of chalk as the heading.

3. Reinforce the concepts by asking for and pointing to the names on the board. For example, ask, "What's your middle name?" and point to the student's middle name as well as the word *Middle* at the column head.

4. Distribute handout 64. Explain that students are to look at the word at the left, find the same word in the group of words beside it, and circle that word. Go over the example, explaining the

concept of "same" and "different." It is essential that the student be able to distinguish these. If this is not clear to the student, use other examples to help the student understand the distinction. The other words presented are real words. Students at this level generally don't ask about the other words.

After correct completion of the top part of the handout, instruct students to match the words that are the same in the bottom part. Each word appears in both uppercase and lowercase forms.

5. Next, distribute handout 65. At the top of the handout, write the student's complete name, first name, middle name, and last name on the appropriate lines. Instruct the student to copy. Carefully monitor each student's progress; if a student is having difficulty in completing the handout, tutor him or her. Work with students individually. A name card could be made for each student on a large sheet of colored paper, as follows:

NAME	*Hae*	*Ja*	*Park*
	First	Middle	Last

NAME	*Mee*		*Thao*
	First	Middle	Last

Students could keep these cards on their desks to copy from.

6. Distribute handouts 66–69, giving each student the next handout only after successful completion of the previous one.

7. Distribute handout 70. Explain to students that *MI* is the short way to write *Middle Initial* and that this signifies the writing of only the first letter of the middle name. Work with students individually, writing the student's middle initial (if the student has a middle name) on the handout and having the student copy it. Then tell students to write the information needed to complete the handout.

8. Distribute handout 71. Direct students to write their first, middle, and last names as indicated on the lines at the top of the handout and then full names on the lines at the bottom of the page. Call attention to the It's Your Cue exercise and tell students they are to complete the sentence.

9. Print students' names on large sheets of colored paper, each name on a separate sheet. Write all the first names on blue paper, the middle names on yellow paper, and the last names on purple paper. Show students their names on the sheets and ask them to identify their first, middle, and last names.

10. Students should also practice reading other students' names. For further practice, put all the pieces of the students' names in a pile and ask students to find their names.

FOLLOW-UP

1. Using three large sheets of same-colored paper, make facsimiles of forms, as shown below.

   ```
   ┌─────────────────────────────────────┐
   │  _____     │
   │  Name                                │
   └─────────────────────────────────────┘
   ```

   ```
   ┌─────────────────────────────────────┐
   │  _____     │
   │  First        Middle        Last    │
   └─────────────────────────────────────┘
   ```

   ```
   ┌─────────────────────────────────────┐
   │  _____     │
   │  Last         First         Middle  │
   └─────────────────────────────────────┘
   ```

   Point to each word several times and have students repeat the words. Each form may serve as a cue card, indicating to students how they are to respond. Begin by reviewing the name form. Hold the form up and ask each student, "What is your name?" Follow the same procedure with the other forms. After doing this several times, simply hold up a form without asking the question. Students should be able to supply the appropriate information from reading the form. Students may practice doing this together; some students may hold the form and ask the question, and others answer.

2. For conversational practice, name tags may be used. Purchase commercially made name tags that say, "Hello, my name is _____." Have each student write his or her name on the tag and then practice dialogues of introduction, such as the following:

   Rosa: Hello, my name is Rosa.
   Mai: Hello, my name is Mai.
   Rosa: Nice to meet you.
   Mai: Nice to meet you, too.

   Point out the words of the dialogue on the name tags. The advantage here is that students may see some of the words as they say them. As students wear the name tags, they can also see the names of other students. You may also wish to explain the cultural component of an introduction, the handshake.

NOTES Explain that some people do not have a middle name. A student who does not have a middle name may be instructed to respond, "I don't have one" or, "I don't have a middle name" to the question, What's your middle name? Instruct these students to make a dash on the form where *Middle Name, Middle Initial,* or *MI* is designated.

This idea of first, middle, and last names may not be simple for those who are not native English speakers. Some cultures and languages do not use middle names, while some, such as the Hispanic, may use two last names. Vietnamese names are traditionally written in the order of last, middle, and first names.

Many refugees' and immigrants' names are changed as they enter the United States. Because a name is one of the most personal components of self-identity, you must be sensitive to students' feelings regarding the forced change. This name change may be seen in a positive light in that you may use this as a topic for discussion with a student. You may wish to talk with students about how they spelled their names in their home countries, the order in which the names were written, whether the last name was the same as the father's last name, and so on. If students' native languages use a different alphabet, you may ask students to write their names in their native languages. You may also want to ask students to write your name in the students' native alphabets. Most students seem flattered to be asked to do this!

This discussion may also help raise students' self-esteem. By asking questions, you show that the students' native cultures and languages are valued. It is also an opportunity for you to learn. Because of the personal nature of this discussion, it may also help support a bonding between you and your students.

OPTIONAL ACTIVITY

1. As a prelude to handout 73, in which students write the names of their family members, the following vocabulary may be introduced and developed:

father	– mother
husband	– wife
brother	– sister
son	– daughter
grandfather	– grandmother
grandson	– granddaughter

   Distribute handout 72. Students may write the above vocabulary under the appropriate pictures.

   The introduction of this vocabulary and the extent of the activity is left to your discretion. Some students, though at a very beginner level, seem eager to learn this vocabulary and to talk about their families. The family tree can be a source of great pride. The attention of the class members and yourself as students discuss their families can lead to an increase in self-esteem.

   Sometimes members of the same family may be students in the class, such as husband and wife, brother and sister, or father and son. The family tree can be an especially meaningful activity for these students.

2. Distribute handout 73. With this family tree, students have the opportunity to write the names of family members. It is interesting for students to compare their family lines to see how the names are continued. More than that, this activity presents an opportunity for students to share a valuable part of their lives. Each student, with great pride, may use the visual representation to show the history of his or her family.

Some students may not know how to write their family members' names in English or in their native language. Many ESL teachers, after working with certain language groups, come to know the English spelling for foreign names. A more advanced student may also be used to help students in this area.

You may want to ask students to bring photographs of their family members and show the photographs along with the family tree. Opportunities for further language development exist here with the use of *what* and *where* questions. Again, colored paper may be used. For example, on a piece of green paper, print the word *What* and on a piece of orange paper, *Where*. Allow students first to show the picture and say what they want to about it. Then hold up the *What* card and ask, "What is his name?" or "What is her name?" while pointing to the people in the picture. Do the same with the *Where* card: "Where is he?" or "Where is she?" The student may respond, "Thailand," "China," "The United States," and so on. Another student may take the role of teacher and hold the *What* and *Where* cards and ask the questions.

In doing this activity, emotions may surface as students tell of the sadness they feel because family members are living in a distant country or have died because of illness or war injuries. Some students may cry as they show their photographs. In spite of the intense sorrow and grieving that these students must feel, the compassion and concern shown by the other students can be most supportive. This kindness can bring healing to grieving students and provide bonding for all students and yourself. Many students, in spite of their sadness, seem eager and happy to show their family tree and family photographs to other students. Again, students should not be forced to do this. The choice should be left to them.

Students may also seem very interested in your family and may ask you to bring photographs as well. If you do so, you might include a photograph of someone who has died and explain how sad you felt because of the person's death. Explain that even though the person hadn't died because of a war, his or her death nevertheless caused sadness for survivors. Point out that these basic human emotions of love and sadness are what bind all of us together, no matter what our language, country, or race. The ESL class, a place of warmth and comfort, seems an appropriate place to display these emotions. However, if you are uncomfortable with such display of emotion, you may prefer not to engage in these activities.

LESSON 4 Numbers 1–10

OBJECTIVES
1. To understand the concept of number-object relationships.
2. To identify the Arabic numerals as well as their corresponding words.
3. To write the numerals and words.

MATERIALS NEEDED
handouts from blackline masters 74–90
pieces of paper, each with a different number on it
pin-back letters
bulletin board

NEW VOCABULARY

one	four	seven	ten
two	five	eight	How many?
three	six	nine	

INTRODUCTION OF CONCEPT

1. Distribute handout 74. Point to numeral 1 and show the picture of one apple. Continue in this way through number 10.
2. Distribute handout 75, which shows only the numerals. While you say each number, instruct students to point to the number they hear. Go through the numbers in numerical order and then switch to random order.
3. Write the numerals on the board and instruct students to listen while you say each number as you point to the numeral. Have students repeat each word after you. Do this several times in numerical order and then switch to random order.
4. You may remain silent but simply point to a number and have students identify it orally. A student may also do the pointing.
5. While pointing to the pictures of the apples and numbers on handout 74, ask, "How many apples are there?" A student may also ask this question.
6. Count objects in the classroom. "How many students are there?" "How many books are there?" and so on.
7. Say a number and have students put the word on the bulletin board with pin-back letters.
8. Put all the papers with numbers on them in a pile and ask a student to find number 3, 7, and so on. Students could also do this in teams.

READING AND WRITING PRACTICE

1. Distribute handout 76. Instruct students to look at the number at the left and the row of numbers beside it, find the same number in the row, and circle that number. Go over the examples with them.
2. Distribute handout 77 and tell students to match each number with a picture.
3. Distribute handouts 78–82, one at a time. Show students how to follow the arrows to form the numerals correctly. Students may have particular problems with the numerals 4, 5, 7, and 9. Some students may have to do these handouts several times before they can write legible numerals.
4. Distribute handout 83. Point to each numeral and the word below it, saying the number each time. Have students point to the word that is being said.
5. Distribute handout 84. Tell students to look at the number in each row and the words beside it, find the word that is the same as the number, and circle that word.
6. Distribute handout 85. Ask students to match each number and the word for that number.
7. Distribute handouts 86 and 87. Have students copy the word for each number.
8. Distribute handouts 88 and 89. Tell students to write the word for each number. Some students may have difficulty with this and will have to do this exercise several times.
9. Distribute handout 90, the It's Your Cue exercise. Instruct students to write only one number on each line. As you dictate the numbers 1 to 10 in random order, ask students to write the number they hear on one of the lines at the top of the page. Next, tell students to write each number they hear next to the letter they hear. Say, for example, "A, 9" and "B, 3." Continue through the letter J, using all ten numbers.
10. Practice spelling the words aloud, having students dictate the numbers and writing the numerals and words on the board, spelling the words with pin-back letters, and so on.

NOTES Numbers are very difficult for some students to learn in a foreign language. For example, to identify the number five, some students may have to count up to it—"One, two, three, four." Other students may translate from their native language first before identifying the number in English. It may take quite a while for a student to become comfortable with numbers.

Check each student's ability to reproduce the numerals. Some students speak very well in English but write a 9 that looks like a *g*. Others don't put the bottom half on 5.

If you feel it is appropriate, explain the concept of zero. This could be done by making the gesture 0 with the index finger and thumb or in a verbal manner by saying the word *no* before a noun, for example, "No apple." You may also want to use objects in the classroom to illustrate this concept. For example, show a stack of five books. Say, "Five books." Remove the books and then say, "No books" or "Zero books."

LESSON 5 | Telephone Number

OBJECTIVES To read the words *telephone number* and supply the appropriate information in both oral and written forms.

MATERIALS NEEDED handouts from blackline masters 91–93
telephones
area code map of the United States
large sheets of colored paper

NEW VOCABULARY telephone number
phone number
telephone

INTRODUCTION OF CONCEPT

1. Distribute handout 91. Explain that every telephone in use has its own telephone number.
2. Ask individual students, "What's your telephone number?" Have a list of students' names and telephone numbers, since many students may not be able to say their telephone number. This list may be obtained from the registration forms of the students or from family members or friends, who often help new students register.

READING AND WRITING PRACTICE

1. Write each student's name and telephone number on the board. Again review these by asking students individually, "What's your telephone number?" and pointing to it while the student answers.
2. Distribute handout 92. Instruct students to look at the word at the left, find the same word in the group of words beside it, and circle that word. Tell them to match the words that are the same at the bottom of the handout.
3. Distribute handout 93. Sit down with students individually and write the student's area code and telephone number on the handout the first time it is indicated. Tell the student to copy the information.
4. To help explain *Area Code,* use the map of the United States with area codes marked in. Show students their city and its area code. Explain that area code is used only for making telephone calls to places that are far away. Students may be familiar with this

from calling their home country or country of residence before coming to the United States.

5. Using a large sheet of colored paper, make a telephone card for each student as follows:

TELEPHONE NUMBER _____
Area Code   Telephone

Students could keep these cards at their desks to copy from.

FOLLOW-UP

A student may go to the board to take the role of teacher. This student may ask other students individually, "What's your telephone number?" and then write the number on the board. Have students take turns being teacher and student. This exercise provides listening as well as pronunciation practice.

NOTES Caution students not to give information such as their name and address over the telephone. Explain that they are under no obligation to supply this information to strangers.

After completing the lessons on address and telephone number, you may wish to have students use their newly acquired skills in a lesson on safety. They might practice calling the fire and police departments and supplying essential information such as name, address, and telephone number over the telephone.

LESSON 6 | Social Security Number

OBJECTIVES
1. To understand the significance of a Social Security number.
2. To read the words *Social Security Number* and supply the appropriate information in written and oral forms.

MATERIALS NEEDED
handouts from blackline masters 94–96
Social Security cards of students
large sheets of colored paper

NEW VOCABULARY
Social Security
number

INTRODUCTION OF CONCEPT

1. Distribute handout 94. Explain that the illustration is of a Social Security card and point out the words SOCIAL SECURITY and NUMBER on the card. Call attention to the fact that the number is missing on the Social Security card.

2. Ask students to show their Social Security cards.

3. Working with students individually, point out on their cards the words SOCIAL SECURITY and NUMBER and their specific number. Practice with each student the pronunciation of the number. Ask students to write their Social Security number on handout 94 in the place indicated.

READING AND WRITING PRACTICE

1. Distribute handout 95. Tell students to look at the word at the left, find the same word in the group of words beside it, and circle that word. Ask them to match the words that are the same at the bottom of the handout.

2. Distribute handout 96. Sit down with students individually and write the student's Social Security number on the first line of the handout. Instruct the student to copy the number as indicated on the handout and complete the It's Your Cue exercise.

3. On a large sheet of colored paper, make a Social Security number card for each student as follows:

| SOCIAL SECURITY NUMBER | -- | -- |

Students could keep these cards on their desks to copy from.

FOLLOW-UP

Ask each student, "What is your Social Security number?"

NOTES It is suggested that you have a list of all students' Social Security numbers in case they forget to bring their cards to school. This information is usually available from school registration forms. Inform students that they should be careful with their cards and should either keep them in their wallets or keep the original in a safe place in their homes and carry a copy in their wallets.

CHECKUP 1

Before distributing handout 97, Checkup 1, review the previous lessons using the cue cards for name, telephone number, and Social Security number. As before, ask questions while showing the cue card. Have students take the various roles of asking the questions, answering, holding the cue card, and so on.

Distribute Checkup 1 and ask students to write in the appropriate information. If a student has great difficulty in completing the Checkup, you may want to give the student the handouts for the particular problem area. For example, if a student has difficulty in writing his or her phone number, give the appropriate handouts to the student and tutor him or her until the student is able to write the telephone number without difficulty.

LESSON 7 | Numbers 11–19

OBJECTIVES
1. To identify the Arabic numerals as well as their corresponding words.
2. To write the numerals and words.

MATERIALS NEEDED
handouts from blackline masters 98–109
bingo game

NEW VOCABULARY

eleven	fourteen	seventeen
twelve	fifteen	eighteen
thirteen	sixteen	nineteen

REVIEW

Review the numbers from one to ten. This can be done by writing the numbers on the board and asking students to identify them, holding up fingers and having students tell the number shown, writing a number and then having students say or write the number that follows, and so on. Any of the activities from Lesson 4, Numbers 1–10, may serve as review activities.

INTRODUCTION OF CONCEPT

1. Distribute handout 98. Say each number and have students point to the number they hear. Say the numbers in numerical order and then in random order.
2. Write each numeral on the board and ask students to identify it.
3. Count objects in the classroom. Ask, "How many students are there?" "How many desks are there?" "How many books are there?" and so on.
4. After you model the activity, have a student come to the front of the class and hold up fingers while the other students identify the number shown.

READING AND WRITING PRACTICE

1. Distribute handout 99 and ask students to look at the number at the left, find the same number in the group beside it, and circle that number.

2. Distribute handout 100. Discuss the spellings of the words and spell the words aloud.

3. Distribute handout 101. Have students look at the number at the left, find the word for that number at the right, and then circle the word that is the same as the number.

4. Distribute handout 102. Tell students to match each number and the word for that number.

5. Distribute handouts 103–105. Have students copy the words for the numbers.

6. Distribute handout 106. Ask students to fill in the missing letter or letters.

7. Distribute handout 107. Have students write the missing numbers and their corresponding words.

8. Distribute handouts 108 and 109. Ask students to write the word for each numeral.

FOLLOW-UP

1. Have students tell the number that comes before a specified number. For example, say "Five"; students should answer, "Four." Repeat with numbers that come *after*. Then ask questions on *between*: "What number is between eight and ten?" Students should answer, "Nine." This activity may be too difficult for some students; if so, do not continue.

2. Go around the room, having each person say a sequential number. For example, have the first student say, "One," the next student, "Two," the next "Three." Do it again going in the opposite direction or having a different student start with number one.

3. Play number bingo. One student may be the caller, while the others play their cards. Students may take turns being the caller. The excitement is increased if prizes are awarded!

4. To make the numbers more relevant and personal, ask these questtions:

   How many children do you have?
   How many brothers and sisters do you have?
   How many people are there in your family?
   How many people live in your house?
   How many students are there in our class?
   How many teachers are there in our class?
   How many men are there in our class?
   How many women are there in our class?
   How many children are there in our class?

NOTES Be aware that some students may reply to the question, How many people are there in your family? with numbers such as twenty or thirty. In some cultures, members count all cousins, aunts, uncles, and other relatives as "family." This can lead to interesting class discussions about what constitutes a family. You may want to mention that in the United States we often think of family as "immediate family, or only the closest relatives."

The question, How many people live in your house? can also be interesting. Students could compare how many people live in their house in the United States with how many people lived in their house in their home country. Explain that in the United States some people live alone—one person in one house. For many students the idea of someone living alone is quite foreign.

Many students like to talk about their families and indeed are very willing to discuss their lives in their home country, but in some instances, where family members have died, there may still be great sadness and sense of loss. It is important that you show sensitivity and use discretion in dealing with such situations and proceed according to what you are comfortable with and what you judge to be in the best interest of the student.

LESSON 8 | Numbers 20–100

OBJECTIVES
1. To identify the Arabic numerals as well as their corresponding words.
2. To write the numerals and words.

MATERIALS NEEDED
handouts from blackline masters 110–120
notebook paper
pin-back numbers
bulletin board

NEW VOCABULARY

twenty	forty	sixty	eighty
twenty-one	forty-one	sixty-one	eighty-one
twenty-two	forty-two	sixty-two	eighty-two
twenty-three	forty-three	sixty-three	eighty-three
twenty-four	forty-four	sixty-four	eighty-four
twenty-five	forty-five	sixty-five	eighty-five
twenty-six	forty-six	sixty-six	eighty-six
twenty-seven	forty-seven	sixty-seven	eighty-seven
twenty-eight	forty-eight	sixty-eight	eighty-eight
twenty-nine	forty-nine	sixty-nine	eighty-nine
thirty	fifty	seventy	ninety
thirty-one	fifty-one	seventy-one	ninety-one
thirty-two	fifty-two	seventy-two	ninety-two
thirty-three	fifty-three	seventy-three	ninety-three
thirty-four	fifty-four	seventy-four	ninety-four
thirty-five	fifty-five	seventy-five	ninety-five
thirty-six	fifty-six	seventy-six	ninety-six
thirty-seven	fifty-seven	seventy-seven	ninety-seven
thirty-eight	fifty-eight	seventy-eight	ninety-eight
thirty-nine	fifty-nine	seventy-nine	ninety-nine
			one hundred

REVIEW

1. Review the numbers 1–19 by using any of the activities from Lessons 4 and 7.
2. Write the numeral, word, or both on the board for the numbers 1–19 and ask students to identify them.

INTRODUCTION OF CONCEPT

Distribute handout 110, which shows numerals only. Instruct students to point to each number while you say it. Say all the numbers in numerical order and then switch to random order.

READING AND WRITING PRACTICE

1. Distribute handout 111 and instruct students to look at the number at the left, find the same number in the group of numbers beside it, and circle that number.
2. Distribute handout 112 and tell students to write in the missing numbers.
3. Distribute handouts 113–115, which show the numerals and words. Say each word while students point to the numeral and word on the handout. Discuss the spellings of the words and the fact that many of them are hyphenated. Students may dictate numbers to you. Write both the numeral and the word on the board. Or students, in turn, may take the role of teacher and write the numerals and words on the board as other students dictate them.
4. Distribute handout 116 and ask students to match each number with the word.
5. For added practice, students may write the numerals and words in their notebooks. It may take some time for students to feel confident in spelling all the numbers.
6. Distribute handouts 117–120. Have students write in the missing numerals and words.

FOLLOW-UP

1. Play Buzz. Say, "One." Then go around the room and have each person say the next number in sequence. Tell students that if their number has the number seven in it, as in seven, seventeen, twenty-seven, and thirty-seven, they should say "Buzz" instead of the number itself. (Example: 15, 16, buzz, 18, 19 . . .) Have students stand and if they miss "buzz," sit down. Award prizes to the students still standing when you call time. Change the numbers from time to time.
2. Play number bingo.
3. Use pin-back numbers in a dictation. Ask students to pin the dictated number on the bulletin board.

NOTES If possible, obtain a desk-top calculator with large-size buttons. This gives the added advantage of allowing students to "touch" the numbers. Or, suggest to students that they purchase pocket-size calculators. This depends, of course, on the financial ability of the students.

You may also want to obtain a beginning math program on computer. Be alert to the level of the language in the program as well as the clarity of the graphics.

Many students are very interested in math, and after learning the numbers in English, they can begin to use them in mathematical calculations such as addition, subtraction, multiplication, and division. The level of these calculations would depend on the educational background of the student. The calculator could be used here. Students could also be introduced to the accompanying vocabulary of *plus, minus, equals, times, multiplied by,* and *divided by.* Even though students may know how to do these calculations in their own language, they often seem intrigued to use the vocabulary in English.

You may also wish to begin a unit on money after students learn the numbers.

LESSON 9 | Address—Number and Street

OBJECTIVES
1. To understand the concept of address and that each place of residence has a distinct number.
2. To read the words *address, number,* and *street* as well as the abbreviations *St.* and *No.*

MATERIALS NEEDED
handouts from blackline masters 121–128
colored chalk
large sheets of colored paper
city map
pin-back letters
bulletin board

NEW VOCABULARY

address	number	south	west	apartment
street	north	east	house	flat

REVIEW

Write the word *Name* on the board and the headings *Address, Number,* and *Street* in different-colored chalk, as in the following:

Name (orange)		Address (green)
	Number (white)	Street (pink)
Mae Her	1310	S. 21 Street
Inthavy Bounyang	2629	W. State Street

Ask each student to spell her or his name as you write it on the board. Ask, "What's your address?" and write the information under Number and Street. You should have a list of students' names and addresses, since many students may not be able to tell their address. The question may serve as a diagnostic tool. Some students may be able to say their address but not be certain about writing it; others may be unable to say it or write it.

INTRODUCTION OF CONCEPT

1. Use the picture on handout 121 to show that each place of residence has a different number. Point out the number of the house or apartment and the name of the street. The terms *house, apartment,* and *flat* may also be introduced and discussed by asking, "Do you live in a house or an apartment [flat]?"
2. Explain that *address* means "number" and "street," that "number" is the number that is on the house or apartment building and

that "street" is the name of the street where the house or apartment building is.

3. Using the picture on handout 122, show the directions of north, south, east, and west. A world map could be used to show the location of countries; for example, Vietnam is in the East and the United States in the West. A map of students' current city of residence could also be used to show directions. You may also wish to point out to students the locations of their home addresses on the local map. Explain to students that the short way to write *North* is *N.*, the short way to write *South* is *S.*, and so on.

READING AND WRITING PRACTICE

1. Distribute handouts 123 and 124. Explain that students are to look at the word at the left, find the same word in the group of words beside it, and circle that word. Point out that at the bottom of the page, students are to match the words.

2. Distribute handout 125. Instruct students to copy. Again, explain that *N.* is the short way to write *North, S.* is the short way to write *South,* and so on.

3. Distribute handout 126. Write each student's house number on the handout and instruct the student to copy. Do the same with the street name.

4. Distribute handout 127. Write the number and street on the address form for each student and have the student copy.

5. Distribute handout 128. Have students write the information asked for and then complete the It's Your Cue exercise.

FOLLOW-UP

1. Using large sheets of colored paper, write the vocabulary, as shown below. All the sheets should be in the same color.

```
┌─────────────────────────┐
│  _____    │
│  Address                │
└─────────────────────────┘

┌─────────────────────────┐
│  _____    │
│  Number                 │
└─────────────────────────┘

┌─────────────────────────┐
│  _____    │
│  Street                 │
└─────────────────────────┘
```

```
┌─────────────────────────────────────────────┐
│   Address ─────────────────────────────     │
│            Number              Street       │
└─────────────────────────────────────────────┘
```

The students should be able to read the words after completing the reading and writing exercises. The sheets may serve as cue cards, indicating to students how they are to answer. Begin by reviewing the Number and Street cards with students. While holding up the Address card, ask, "What is your address?" After doing this several times, simply hold up the card without asking the question. Students should be able to answer appropriately from reading the card. Students may practice doing this together, with some students holding the cue cards and asking the questions and other students answering.

2. Print each student's address on large pieces of paper in the same color as that used for the cue cards—the number on one sheet and the street on another. Put all numbers and streets in a pile and ask students to find their address and show it, as well as say it, to the class.

3. Students can ask each other, "What is your address?" and answer, "My address is _____." The student who asks the question could then write the address on the board. A review of the alphabet may be necessary, since some students may have to spell the name of their street.

4. Repeat procedure 3, but instead of writing on the board, have students "write" the addresses with pin-back letters.

NOTES You may want to ask students what their address was in their home country. This could lead to an interesting discussion, since some students may have lived in small villages and not had an address per se.

Again, using the local city map, help students locate their address and pinpoint it with a colored marker. In this way, then, each student's home is designated. This map could be hung in the classroom.

You may want to print a card for each student with her or his address on it so that the student may have this to copy from.

WORD SEARCH 1

Distribute handout 129. Review the vocabulary with students and instruct them to look for the words in the puzzle. Explain that the words may be written either from left to right or from top to bottom.

Since this may be a new activity for students, you may want to do the entire activity with the group.

ANSWER KEY

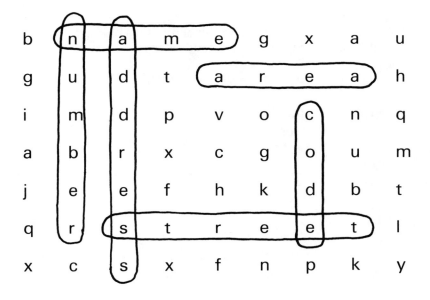

LESSON 10 | Address—City, State, and Zip Code

OBJECTIVES
1. To understand the significance of city, state, and zip code in an address.
2. To recognize the words *city, state,* and *zip code* and supply the correct information in written and oral forms.

MATERIALS NEEDED
handouts from blackline masters 130–136
map of the United States
city map
large sheets of colored paper

NEW VOCABULARY
city
state
zip code

REVIEW

1. Review the previous lesson on address by asking, "What is your address?" As students respond, indicate again students' addresses on the local city map.

INTRODUCTION OF CONCEPT

1. Call attention to the map of the United States. Distribute handout 130. Explain that the United States is composed of fifty states and many cities. Explain that there are also many small towns and country villages that are referred to as cities. Show students where their current residence is by indicating city and state and have them write the name of each in the appropriate place on the map.
2. Use the city map again to show how the city is divided into zip code areas. Help students locate their zip codes.

READING AND WRITING PRACTICE

1. Distribute handout 131. Ask students to look at the word at the left, find the same word in the group of words beside it, and circle that word. Then have students match the words at the bottom of the handout.

2. Write the word *City* on the board and next to it write the name of the city of residence. Do the same with *State*. While writing, discuss the spellings of the names.

3. Distribute handout 132. On each student's handout, write the name of the city on the first line and instruct students to copy the information on the following lines.

   Repeat procedure 3 with the name of the state.
   Repeat procedure 3 with the zip code.

4. Distribute handouts 133 and 134. Ask students to fill in the information.

5. Distribute handout 135, in which students are to draw on previously learned material, address, and put this in context with the newly learned city, state, and zip code.

6. Distribute handout 136, the It's Your Cue exercise. Ask students to complete the sentences.

FOLLOW-UP

1. Using large sheets of colored paper, make cue cards as shown below.

   ```
   _____
         City
   ```

   ```
   _____
         State
   ```

   ```
   _____
        Zip Code
   ```

   ```
   _____
   City    State    Zip Code
   ```

   All cards should be of the same color paper. Pointing to each word, say it and have students repeat the word after you. Use the papers as cue cards and have students ask each other appropriate questions, for example, "What city do you live in?"

2. On three separate pieces of colored paper, write the city, state, and zip code of each student and put these in a pile. Ask students to

"find" their address. Another variation is to have students take the first address card they choose and say the city, state, or zip code aloud. A student who has the same city, state, or zip code must respond.

3. You might also ask students to write the information on the board or with pin-back letters.

4. Have students practice asking each other these questions:

What city do you live in?
What state do you live in?
What's your zip code?
And for review: What's your address?

NOTES You may also want to discuss the concept of "country" (this will be dealt with more extensively in Lesson 16). Students' city and state or province in the home country can also be discussed. Ask, for example, "What was your city?" or "What was your state?"

Students may have relatives living in other cities in the United States. This could also be discussed. Ask such questions as these:

Where does your sister live?
What city does your brother live in?
What state does your cousin live in?

WORD SEARCH 2

Distribute handout 137. Tell students to find the words in the puzzle and circle them. Remind students that words can be written either from left to right or from top to bottom.

ANSWER KEY

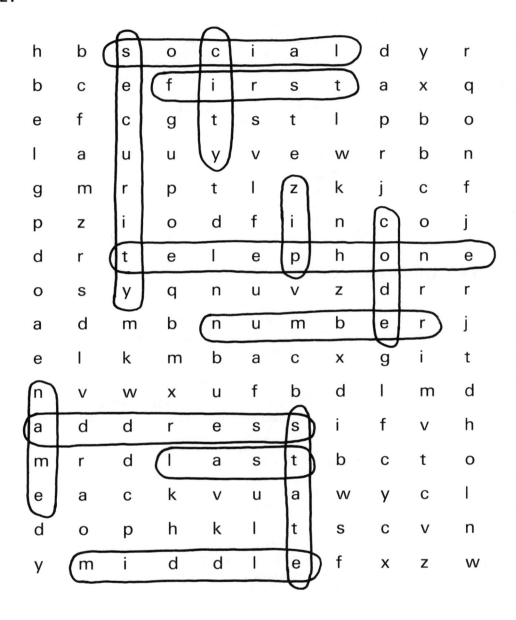

CHECKUP 2

Distribute handout 138. Again, use the cue cards to review the items on Checkup 2. If a student has difficulty with an item on the Checkup, tutor her or him and when appropriate readminister the Checkup.

LESSON 11 | Marital Status

OBJECTIVES
1. To understand the meaning of the term *marital status* and identify a particular status.
2. To identify appropriate terms for marital status in both oral and written forms.

MATERIALS NEEDED
handouts from blackline masters 139–143
pin-back letters
bulletin board

NEW VOCABULARY
single   separated
married   widowed
divorced

INTRODUCTION OF CONCEPT

1. Distribute handout 139. Point to each picture and say the name of the marital state shown: single, married, separated, divorced, and widowed. Students may have difficulty distinguishing between "separated" and "divorced." Explain that when people are divorced, they are given a paper from the court that says that they are no longer married.
2. Discuss the marital status of the students in the class. Ask students, "Are you single?" "Are you married?"

READING AND WRITING PRACTICE

1. Distribute handout 140. Direct students to look at the word at the left, find the same word in the group of words beside it, and circle that word. Then have them match the words at the bottom of the handout.
2. Distribute handout 141, which shows pictures and words. Write the terms for marital status on the board and discuss the spelling of each.
3. Distribute handout 142. Advise students that ☐ implies making an X or ✔ in the box and that a line implies making a ✔. Explain that they can mark only one box or one line.
4. Distribute handout 143. Write each student's marital status on the first line and ask the student to copy the status. Have students complete the It's Your Cue exercise at the bottom of the handout.
5. Have students write their marital status with pin-back letters.

FOLLOW-UP

1. While pointing to the picture on handout 141, ask students, "Are you single?" "Are you married?" Have students ask each other.
2. Point to a student and ask other class members, "Is he [she] married?"
3. Expanded questions include, "Is your brother [sister] married?" "When did you get married?" "Where did you get married?"

NOTES Discussion of marital status can be very entertaining! Students can share information regarding customs of courtship and marriage in their cultures; these customs can also be explained as they exist in the United States. The extent of this discussion depends on the level of the students. Some students, even though at a beginner level, enjoy a discussion of this sort because it deals with something they know about and provides them with an opportunity to share something of their culture.

Some students are embarrassed to say that they are divorced, and others have painful memories regarding becoming widowed. Sensitivity on your part is crucial here. The warmth of the classroom environment can support a student in what could be a difficult situation.

LESSON 12 | Sex

OBJECTIVES
1. To understand that the terms *male* and *female* are designated by the word *Sex* on a form.
2. To understand the terms *male* and *female* and identify them in both oral and written forms.

MATERIALS NEEDED   handouts from blackline masters 144–146

NEW VOCABULARY
Sex
male
female

REVIEW

Point to various students and designate them as man or woman. Then point to a student and have other students say, "Man" or "Woman."

INTRODUCTION OF CONCEPT

Distribute handout 144. Use the illustration to show the meaning of the terms *Male* and *Female*. Explain that *woman* signifies "female" and *man* signifies "male."

READING AND WRITING PRACTICE

1. Write *Male* and *Female* on the board and discuss the spelling of each word.
2. Distribute handout 145. Direct students to look at the word at the left, find the same word in the group of words beside it, and circle that word. Then have them match the words at the bottom of the handout.
3. Distribute handout 146. Instruct students to follow the directions and either circle or check each correct answer. Then write each student's sex on the first line at the bottom of the handout and instruct him or her to copy.

FOLLOW-UP

1. Point to individual students in the class and ask others, "Male or female?" Say various words that designate a particular sex and ask

the same question. For example, if you say, "Grandmother," the class should respond, "Female." If you say, "Son," the response should be "Male."

2. Use these questions for discussion:
   How many males [females] are there in your family?
   How many males [females] live in your house?
   How many males [females] are there in our classroom?

NOTES Students should recognize the fact that this question may appear in different ways on a form. Sometimes they will have to circle a word, circle an abbreviation, put an X or a ✔ in a box, or make a check on a line next to a word.

LESSON 13 | Formal Titles

OBJECTIVES To recognize titles and use them correctly in oral and written forms.

MATERIALS NEEDED handouts from blackline masters 147–148

NEW VOCABULARY
Mr.   Mrs.
Ms.   Miss

REVIEW

Review the concepts of male and female, using any of the activities from Lesson 12.

INTRODUCTION OF CONCEPT

1. Point to a married male student and designate him as "Mr." Point to a single male student and do the same. Indicate a married female student and designate her as "Mrs." and also as "Ms." Point to a single female student and designate her as "Miss" and also as "Ms." Use each title with the full name: Mr. José Esqueda, Mrs. Mee Thao, Ms. Mee Thao, Miss Trinh Tran, Ms. Trinh Tran.

2. Distribute handout 147 and use the pictures to help explain the formal titles. Point out that titles are different for men and women and that while *Ms.* may be for a married woman as well as for a single woman, *Mrs.* signifies only a married woman and *Miss* only a single woman.

READING AND WRITING PRACTICE

1. Write the titles on the board and discuss the spelling of each, emphasizing that a period must be written with *Mr., Mrs.,* and *Ms.*

2. Work with students individually to show each which title is appropriate.

3. Distribute handout 148. Have students match the titles and then check and circle the appropriate titles. Then ask students to complete the It's Your Cue exercise.

FOLLOW-UP

1. Point to individual students in the class and ask what title is appropriate for each. For example, if a male student is indicated, students should respond, "Mr."
2. Students may practice introductions: "I would like to introduce Ms. Bao Xiong." "I would like to introduce Miss Lao Lee."

NOTES The concepts "Ms." and "Mrs." are difficult for many students to understand. Some students equate *Ms.* with *Miss,* believing that it refers only to an unmarried woman. However, *Ms.* may be the preferred form for many of these students.

For example, in many cultures women do not take their husband's name after marriage. This discrepancy is sometimes difficult for Americans to understand, and thus, the use of *Ms.* may be a way of getting around this difficulty. But again, many students seem to feel that the use of *Ms.* negates their married state. Some single women seem to prefer the use of *Miss* because they believe that that is the only way to designate an unmarried woman. The choice of title should be left to the student, but you can point out how these titles are used and the choices that students have.

You may also mention that in English-speaking countries titles are used formally and to show respect. In some cultures use of the first name is a show of respect, and titles are considered less respectful or not at all respectful.

CHECKUP 3

Distribute handout 149. Use the cue cards and handouts from previous lessons to review for Checkup 3. If a student has difficulty with any item on the Checkup, tutor that student in the particular area of difficulty and readminister the Checkup when appropriate.

WORD SEARCH 3

Distribute handout 150. Review the vocabulary with students and instruct them to find the words in the puzzle and circle them. Remind students that the words may be written either from left to right or from top to bottom.

ANSWER KEY

n	m	a	r	r	i	e	d	f	g
r	a	c	o	u	s	b	i	j	x
t	l	q	z	e	s	m	v	w	r
f	e	m	a	l	e	c	o	h	d
u	y	k	b	c	p	a	r	f	m
s	l	n	e	x	a	n	c	k	n
i	g	v	g	c	r	e	e	b	l
n	f	a	r	g	a	b	d	m	t
g	e	w	q	p	t	i	x	n	y
l	o	y	t	d	e	d	o	g	p
e	u	v	w	i	d	o	w	e	d

38

LESSON 14 | Height and Weight

OBJECTIVES
1. To understand the concepts of height and weight.
2. To understand the U.S. system of measurement in inches, feet, ounces, and pounds.
3. To identify height and weight using U.S. measurements in both oral and written forms.

MATERIALS NEEDED
handouts from blackline masters 151–156
rulers
yardsticks
tape measures
measuring cups
rice or beans
scale

NEW VOCABULARY

inch	foot	ounce	pound
inches	feet	ounces	pounds

INTRODUCTION OF CONCEPT

1. Have two students—one taller than the other—stand up. Move your hand from the feet to the head of each student as you say the word *height*. Ask the other students, "Are they the same or different?"

2. Distribute handout 151. Use the illustration to discuss the concept of height. Show a ruler, yardstick, and tape measure and explain that these are used to measure height. While showing the handout, point to the vertical measure on the scale and the girl and indicate that this is a way of measuring height. Move your hand from your shoes to the top of your head and say that this is the way to measure height. Hold a yardstick next to a student and say, "Height."

3. Using a ruler, show one inch, two inches, and so on, up to twelve inches. Explain that twelve inches equals one foot.

   Make a chart on the board as shown below.

   12 inches = 1 foot
   24 inches = 2 feet
   36 inches = 3 feet
   48 inches = 4 feet
   60 inches = 5 feet
   72 inches = 6 feet

Use the ruler to measure items in the classroom, such as a pencil, a book, and a sheet of paper. Have students use rulers and yardsticks to measure items also.

READING AND WRITING PRACTICE

Distribute handouts 152 and 153. Explain to students that each person in the class will be measured for height. Model the activity first and then have students proceed. Have each student stand against the wall. Two other students may measure, one holding the tape measure at the bottom and another holding it at the top and reading the number (a third student may help read the measurement). A fourth student may write the name of the student and his or her measurements on the board using the format of the chart on handout 152. While the student writes the measurements on the board, the other students may write them on the handout. Students may say the measurement in inches, and the class can determine it using feet and inches. For example, if a student is sixty-four inches tall, her or his height is five feet, four inches. Have students take turns at the various tasks.

Let students also measure you!

FOLLOW-UP

1. After completing the chart, ask individual students, "What is your height?" or "How tall are you?" Have students ask each other the same question.
2. The adjectives *tall* and *short* as well as comparatives may also be discussed. For example, "Is José tall or short?" "Who is the shortest [tallest] person in the class?" Have three students illustrating *tall, taller,* and *tallest* stand together in a line at the front of the class. Do the same with *short, shorter,* and *shortest.*

INTRODUCTION OF CONCEPT

1. Distribute handout 154. Use the pictures to help explain the concept of weight. Use hand gestures and facial expressions to illustrate the idea of heavy and light, or use concrete objects, such as a heavy dictionary and a light paperback, to show the concept. In turn, point to each of the scales and say, "Weight."
2. Explain that in the United States we use ounces and pounds to measure weight.
3. Explain ounces and pounds by using rice or beans. Show them in a box or bag that states the weight. Also, using a measuring cup, show the amount in ounces. Explain that ounces may be used for dry as well as liquid measure but that pounds is used only for dry measure. To illustrate "liquid" and "dry," use water and rice for examples.

READING AND WRITING PRACTICE

1. Distribute handout 155. Using a bathroom scale, have students weigh themselves one at a time. Write the number of pounds on handout 155. Each student should copy the amount on the handout.
2. Distribute handout 156. Have each student write his or her height and weight on the handout and then complete the It's Your Cue exercise.

FOLLOW-UP

1. Ask each student privately, "What is your weight?" or "How much do you weigh?"
2. Explain that when babies are born in the United States, their weight is measured in pounds and ounces. This is referred to as birth weight. Some students may have had children born in the United States, and this information may be of particular interest to them.

NOTES Sensitivity must be exercised when doing the handouts related to height and weight. Some students may be sensitive about their height; others may be sensitive about their weight. Do the weight activities with one student at a time and have each student write her or his own data. In some cultures, weight is not a sensitive issue, and some students may not be embarrassed to discuss it.

Comparisons between U.S. and metric measurements may be helpful to students. You may wish to include more measurements than are given here.

LESSON 15 | Color of Hair and Eyes

OBJECTIVES
1. To identify the colors of hair and eyes and their names in both oral and written forms.
2. To respond appropriately to questions regarding hair and eye color.

MATERIALS NEEDED
handouts from blackline masters 157–160
examples of colors (color cards, colored objects, etc.)
colored magazine photos of people
crayons
colored chalk

NEW VOCABULARY

brown	black	blonde
green	white	hair
blue	gray	eye
red	color	

INTRODUCTION OF CONCEPT

1. Using color cards or other colored objects, show colors to students while naming them. Name the colors for objects in the classroom. Show the magazine photos of people and say, for example, "She has black hair and brown eyes."

2. Distribute handout 157. Point to hair on your head and then to the three heads of hair in the picture, saying the word *hair*. Then ask, "What color is your hair?" as you point to a student. Continue to do this with all students. Follow the same procedure for color of eyes.

READING AND WRITING PRACTICE

1. Distribute handout 158. Direct students to look at the word at the left, find the same word in the group of words beside it, and circle that word. Then have them match the words at the bottom of the handout.

2. On the board write the headings *Color of eyes* and *Color of hair*. Write the appropriate colors under the headings. Explain that brown may be either an eye or hair color.

3. Distribute handout 159. Working with individual students, ask, "What color are your eyes?" and write the response in the appropriate space. Instruct the student to copy. Repeat the procedure with "Color of hair."

4. Distribute handout 160. Tell students to fill in the information asked for and then complete the sentences in the It's Your Cue exercise.

FOLLOW-UP

1. Ask each student, "What color are your eyes?" and "What color is your hair?" Have students ask each other.
2. Additional questions may include these:
   What color are your wife's [husband's, son's, daughter's] eyes?
   What color is your wife's [husband's, son's, daughter's] hair?
3. Indicate a specific student and ask other students, "What color are her [his] eyes?" Do the same with hair color.

NOTES Some students may use *yellow* instead of *blonde* for hair color. Others may use *black* for eye color, for example, "I have black hair and black eyes." Explain that even though their eyes are a very dark color, they are still called brown.

Students can discuss what people in their country look like; for example, people in the northern part have blonde hair and blue eyes, while those in the southern part have black hair and brown eyes. This can lead to a very interesting discussion! Skin color could also be discussed as well as adjectives for hair, such as *straight, curly, short,* and *long.*

Although this lesson focuses on color of hair and eyes, you may wish to introduce other colors as well. One way to do this is to make a circle or line on the board using colored chalk (or on paper using crayons) and ask students to write the name of the color next to the circle or line. Or, write the name of the color on the board with white chalk and ask students to show the color with a piece of chalk or a crayon.

WORD SEARCH 4

Distribute handout 161. Review the vocabulary with students and tell them to circle the words in the puzzle. Explain that the words may be written either from left to right or from top to bottom.

ANSWER KEY

q	b	c	d	o	p	x	y	z	a
x	r	o	u	d	t	y	b	w	x
t	o	b	d	z	k	q	l	l	j
c	w	h	i	t	e	p	o	x	y
o	n	f	r	u	y	i	n	t	k
l	b	m	c	g	e	n	d	s	o
o	j	o	x	b	s	r	e	d	d
r	e	t	b	l	u	e	t	n	b
f	x	g	r	a	y	p	a	j	n
d	e	r	u	c	o	r	t	o	g
x	l	e	w	k	y	h	a	i	r
y	b	e	n	a	r	l	l	n	x
a	v	n	t	s	r	e	t	c	o

LESSON 16 | Place of Birth

OBJECTIVE To identify place of birth in both oral and written forms.

MATERIALS NEEDED
handouts from blackline masters 162–164
world map
colored markers

NEW VOCABULARY
place country
birth origin

INTRODUCTION OF CONCEPT

1. Show the world map and point out different countries, including the home countries of the students. Also show the United States and the city and state of residence.
2. Write the names of students' home countries on the board.
3. Have all students come together to look at the map. Ask each student, "Where are you from?" or "What country are you from?" and locate the country on the map.

READING AND WRITING PRACTICE

1. Make a chart on the board similar to the one below.

Name	Place of Birth
Xao Xiong	Laos
Bounmy Souvannarath	Laos
Nghia Nguyen	Vietnam
José Esqueda	Mexico

2. Explain that *Place of Birth* means the country in which you were born. This idea of "where you were born" is not always the easiest to convey, and you may have to resort to creative mime to help get the point across!
3. Expand on the above chart by adding the term *Country of Origin* as shown below.

Name	Place of Birth	Country of Origin
Xao Xiong	Laos	Laos
Bounmy Souvannarath	Laos	Laos
Nghia Nguyen	Vietnam	Vietnam
José Esqueda	Mexico	Mexico

4. Explain that *Country of Origin* is like *Place of Birth* and ask students, "What is your place of birth?" "What is your country of origin?" Point to the appropriate term while asking the question.

5. Distribute handout 162. Instruct students to look at the word at the left, find the same word in the group of words at the right, and circle that word. Then have them match the words that are the same at the bottom of the handout.

6. Distribute handout 163. Work with students individually. Ask, "What is your place of birth?" and write the name of the country on the first line and instruct the student to copy. After the student has finished copying place of birth, ask the student, "What is your country of origin?" Write the name of the country on the first line and ask the student to again copy the information.

7. Distribute handout 164 and tell students to write the appropriate information and complete the sentence in the It's Your Cue exercise.

FOLLOW-UP

Ask students some of the following questions:

Where are you from?
What is your country?
What is your country of origin?
Where were you born?
What is your place of birth?
What is your nationality?
What is your citizenship?

You may wish to have students respond with short answers or with complete sentences. It is up to you to decide if contractions should be used.

NOTES You may wish to expand on the map activity described on page 45 now to include the city that the student lived in. After pointing to the country, ask the student, "What city did you live in?" and point to various cities within the country. Some students may have difficulty answering this question if they are unable to read a map or do not know the spelling of the name of their city in the Roman alphabet. In this case, you may want to get help from a more advanced student with the same language background. There are, however, some students at the very beginner level who are able and seem most willing to show their home city on a map.

Another map activity is to record each student's journey to the United States. Use the world map and colored markers. Have each student choose a marker in a color that she or he likes. This color will represent the student. Lay the map on a table or desk. Have all students come together and, one at a time, show their home country and then their city in the home country. Using the colored marker, they should make a mark at the location of their city and then continue with a line to their next place of residence, then the next, and so on, until the line ends at their current place of residence in the United States. For example, many students from Laos may show their city in Laos and then how they crossed the Mekong River to go to Thailand. They may then indicate the locations of the various refugee camps in which they lived and their trip to the United States with possible stops in the Philippines, Tokyo, and Hong Kong and then arrival at a U.S. city such as San Francisco or Seattle and finally settlement in a different city. The student may use the marker to make a continuous line from place of birth to current place of residence. For many students, this may be a very long line, showing a journey that has taken them to the other end of the world.

The home country and former locations of residence may be a sensitive subject for many students, considering the trauma that they associate with these places. However, many students like to talk about these places, which have played such a significant role in their lives. Many students want to talk at length about their village, conditions in a refugee camp, their flight to the United States, and so on. This can be a great catalyst for conversation, since students may want to compare notes concerning the proximity of their home cities, relatives who lived in those cities, the refugee camp they were in, and so on.

Many students also seem eager to "teach" others about their homeland. This is a great opportunity for you to ask questions and learn from the students. These questions may be diverse, including such topics as weather and seasons, crops grown and the harvesting of those crops, the money system and its equivalence in U.S. dollars, descriptions of villages and large cities, and languages spoken. The list seems endless! Students can be great teachers, and you can benefit immensely from this new knowledge.

For those students who fled their homeland because of a change in government, politics is a popular topic of discussion. Due to the emotional investment in this subject, students have much to say and may express sadness at the changes that have taken place in their country. Expression of these feelings may be a positive outlet for students, and the warmth of the ESL classroom may provide some comfort for them. Again, your sensitivity and the bonding of class members plays a crucial role.

A map or globe helps students have a visual image of where they fit in the world and may supply those students who have not had a formal education with a representation that, until now, has not been familiar to them. Some students seem to lack an understanding of just how far they've come to get to the United States; there are thousands of miles separating the two places! The map may indicate why many things in this country seem very different from those in their home country. It also allows students to learn about other countries from their classmates.

It is also helpful if you can bring current magazine or newspaper articles about students' home countries to show the class. Videotapes of the home countries are also helpful. Students seem flattered to see that attention has been given to their country in a national or international publication. Looking at the pictures may trigger memories in students that cause them to speak. Some lower-level students may not be able to verbalize, but you may read their faces. Many of them will respond in a nonverbal manner.

LESSON 17 Age

OBJECTIVE To state one's age correctly in both oral and written forms.

MATERIALS NEEDED handouts from blackline masters 165–166

NEW VOCABULARY age
years
old

REVIEW

Review some of the personal information questions from previous lessons, such as, What is your height? What color is your hair? What color are your eyes? Are you married or single? Have students practice asking each other the questions.

INTRODUCTION OF CONCEPT

Distribute handout 165. Use the pictures on the handout to illustrate the concept of age. Discuss the ages of the people in the picture. Students may not all agree on the ages!

READING AND WRITING PRACTICE

1. Write the word *age* on the board and explain that it means how many years a person has lived. A review of numbers may be appropriate here.

2. Write the words *Name* and *Age* on the board as column headings. Ask each student, "What is your age?" and then write the student's name and response on the board as shown below.

Name	*Age*
Ye Yang	21
Noo Vang	20

    Discuss the fact that the response to "What is your age?" is "I am ____ years old" and that we don't usually say, "My age is ____."

3. Distribute handout 166. Tell students to write their age on the lines and check the appropriate box. Then have them complete the sentence in the It's Your Cue exercise.

FOLLOW-UP

1. Explain that the questions What is your age? and How old are you? are interchangeable. Ask both questions of students and then have them ask each other.

2. Another question that could be asked is, What year were you born?

3. The ages of students' family members could also be discussed, for example, "How old is your son [daughter]?" "How old is your husband [wife]?" "How old is your mother [father]?"

4. To the question, "How old are you?" the response is, "I am ____ years old." Write the phrase *years old* on the board so that students may see it as they answer.

NOTES The adjectives *old* and *young* may also be used here.

Some students—such as the Hmong, who come from a society in which written records are not kept—may not be sure of their exact birth date and thus may not know their true age. Upon entering the United States, a birth date is usually assigned to them, and this date appears on all their documentation.

For safety reasons, some students have had to take on an assumed identity and for this reason do not profess their true age; some students might confess this to you. Again, your sensitivity is crucial.

Different cultures may have different ways of actually counting the years for an age. This can lead to an interesting discussion!

LESSON 18 Date of Birth, Date of Arrival, and Today's Date

OBJECTIVES
1. To understand the arrangement of time, as in calendar time, in the Western calendar.
2. To identify dates in both oral and written forms.
3. To present correctly in both oral and written forms date of birth, date of arrival in the United States, and today's date.

MATERIALS NEEDED handouts from blackline masters 167–189
twelve-month calendar for the current year

NEW VOCABULARY

month	January	April	July	October	today's date
year	February	May	August	November	date of birth
date	March	June	September	December	date of arrival

INTRODUCTION OF CONCEPT

1. Show the twelve-month calendar and explain that twelve months is equal to one year. Write the words *month, year,* and *date* on the board while showing a month on the calendar and then a particular date.
2. Identify the names of the months.
3. Write on the board particular dates, such as January 1, 1989, while showing them on the calendar. Continue to illustrate different dates and be sure to include the day's date.

READING AND WRITING PRACTICE

1. Distribute handout 167. Instruct students to look at the word at the left, find the same word in the group of words beside it, and circle that word. Ask them to match the words at the bottom of the handout.
2. Distribute handout 168. Explain that each month also has a number. Have students practice saying the names of the months.
3. Discuss the spellings of the names of the months and have students practice writing the names on the board and spelling them orally.
4. While students look at their handout, hold up one finger and ask, "What is the first month of the year?" At this level, students will most likely be unfamiliar with ordinal numbers, and designating the number with fingers might help them understand. Proceed

like this with the rest of the months in sequence and then in random order.

5. Distribute handouts 169-171 and ask students to copy the numbers and names of the months.

6. Distribute handout 172 and instruct students to match the number of each month with the name.

7. Distribute handout 173 and explain to students that they are to fill in the missing letters for the names of the months.

8. Using the calendar, show a specific date while writing it on the board. Identify the month, day, and year as shown below.

    July   27,   1989
   Month   Day   Year

Distribute handout 174 and provide additional examples on the board.

9. Distribute handout 175. Discuss the example and have students circle the date that is shown on the calendar at the bottom of the handout. Then distribute handouts 176 and 177 and instruct students to circle each date that is the same as the one circled on the calendar.

10. Distribute handouts 178 and 179. Ask students to complete the calendars. You will have to pay attention to those months that have thirty-one days. Students most probably will not have made this distinction yet.

11. Show the calendar for the current month. Review with students the name of the month, the year, and when the first day of the month occurs. Distribute handout 180 and tell students to put in the dates to fill in the calendar. After completion, have students circle today's date.

12. Write the words *Date of Birth* and *Birth Date* on the board and explain that these groups of words mean the same thing. Explain that this is the day a person was born.

13. Write the words *Date of Arrival* on the board and explain that this is the date students came to the United States.

14. Distribute handout 181. Sit down with students individually and write their date of birth on the handout. Ask them to copy. Do the same with date of arrival.

15. Distribute handout 182. Tell students to fill in the information indicated.

16. Review handout 168, which shows the months and their numbers. Distribute handout 183. Explain that December is the twelfth month of the year, so it can be written with the number 12. The date is the twelfth day of the month, and this is written as the number 12. The year is 1989, but when writing a date with numbers only, we only need to write the last two numbers, not *19*. This may be explained as the short way to write a date.

17. Distribute handouts 184 and 185. Call attention to handout 184. Ask students, "What's the date?" Discuss the date of November 18, 1989, and how to write it using only numbers. Instruct students to circle the correct date on the calendar (here 18). Repeat the procedure with handout 185.

18. Distribute handouts 186 and 187. Write the first few dates on the board with numbers and discuss them with students. Then instruct students to complete the handouts.

19. Distribute handout 188 and tell students to write the appropriate information in the spaces. For review, have handout 181 (students wrote the information with words) nearby.

20. Distribute handout 189. Using the calendar for the current month, write the date the long way on the board and then ask students to supply the date using numbers. Instruct them to write today's date on the handout and then complete the sentences in the It's Your Cue exercise.

FOLLOW-UP

1. Using the calendar, identify the months orally and have students repeat.

2. Identify the months with numbers. For example, say, "Four" (or show the number four with your fingers) and have students respond, "April." Do the reverse as well.

3. Pointing to the calendar, ask as follows:
   How many days are there in April?
   How many days are there in May?

   Continue with the remaining months.

4. Spell the names of the months orally while writing them on the board.

5. Ask questions such as the following:

   What is your birth date?
   What is your date of birth?
   When were you born?
   When did you arrive in the United States?

   Students will not be familiar with the past tense, but a lengthy explanation is not needed.

NOTES Because days of the week are not an essential part of birth date and date of arrival, they have not been included in this lesson. You may choose to add days of the week to the lesson.

CHECKUPS 4-8

Distribute handouts 190-194 in numerical order one at a time. These are the final Checkups. As before, if a student has difficulty with a particular concept, tutor him or her and readminister the Checkup when appropriate.

LESSON 1 Visual Discrimination

Circle the shape that is different.

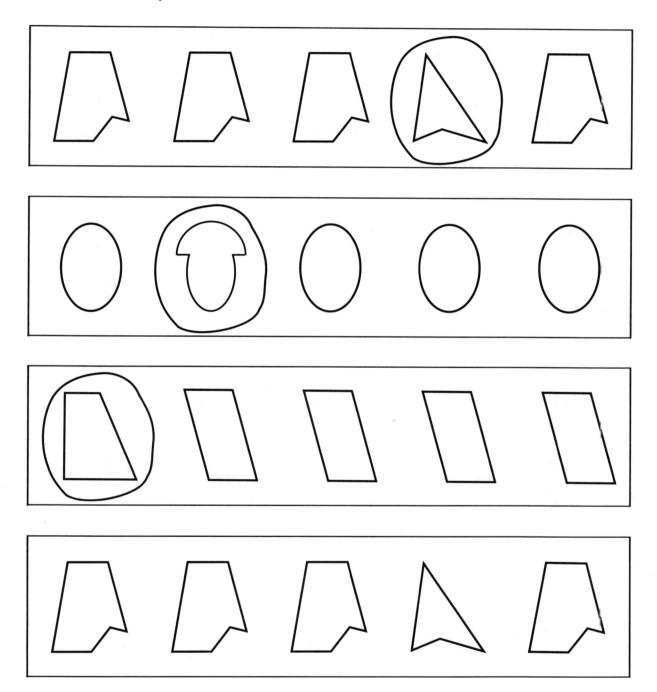

LESSON 1 Visual Discrimination

Circle the shape that is different.

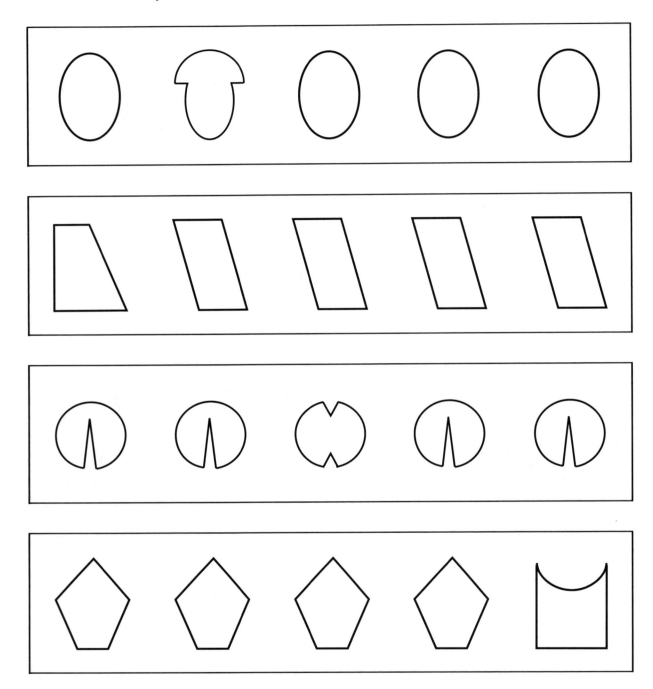

LESSON 1 Visual Discrimination

Circle the shape that is the same.

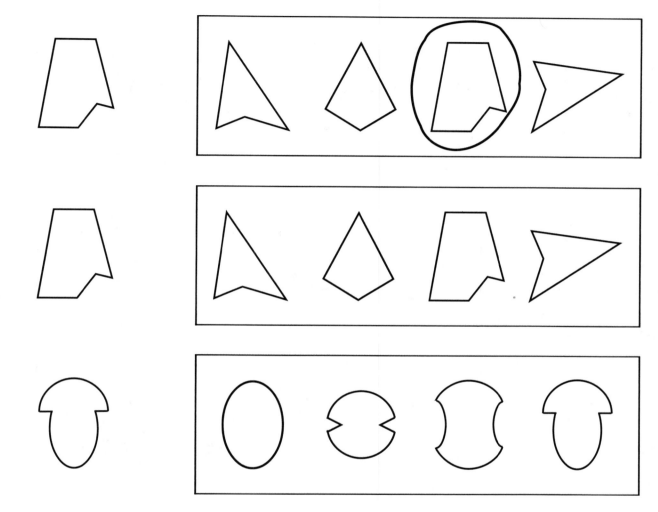
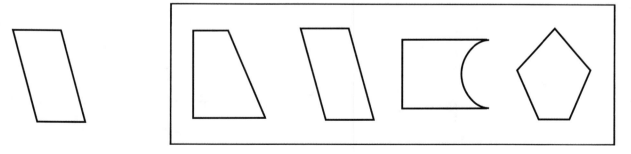
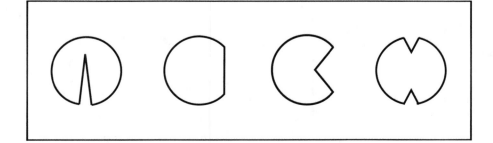

LESSON 1 Visual Discrimination

Circle the shape that is the same.

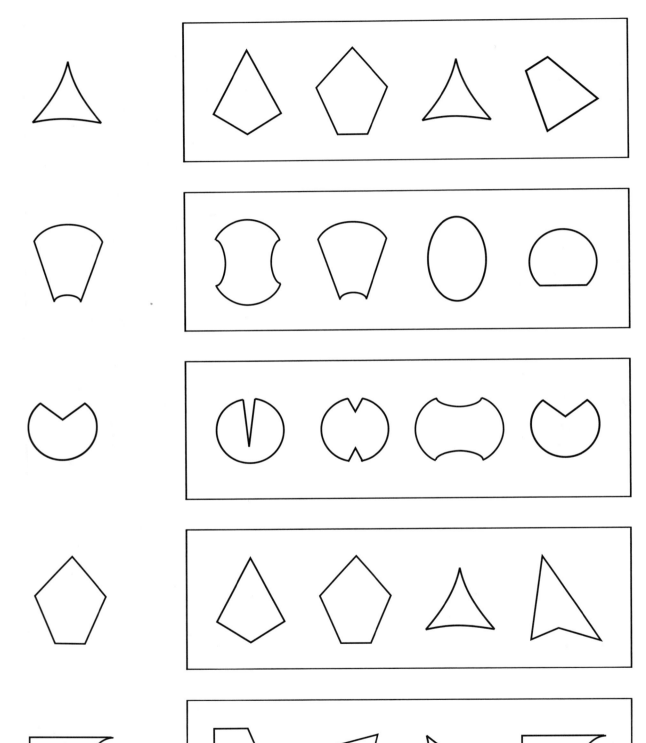

LESSON 1 Visual Discrimination

Match the shapes.

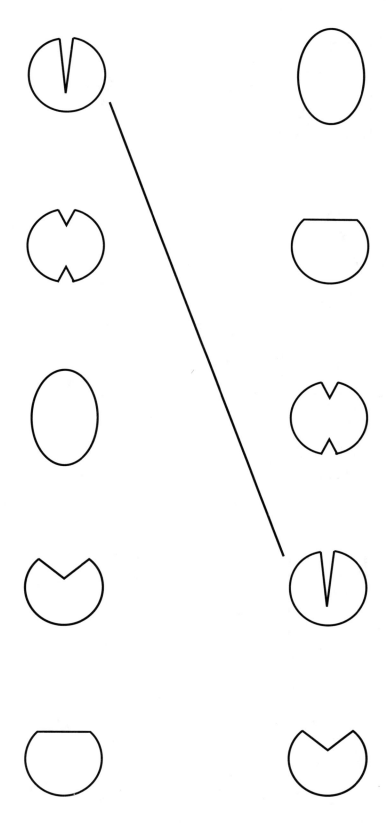

LESSON 1 Visual Discrimination

Match the shapes.

 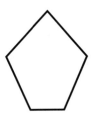

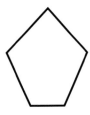 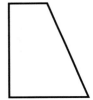

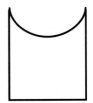

LESSON 1 Visual Discrimination

7

Circle the shape that is different.

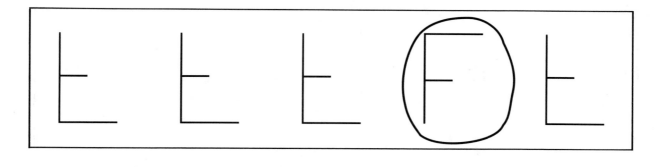

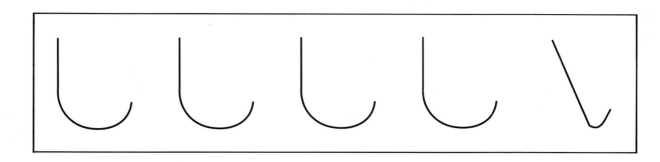

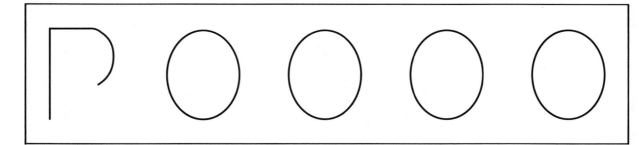

LESSON 1 Visual Discrimination

Circle the shape that is different.

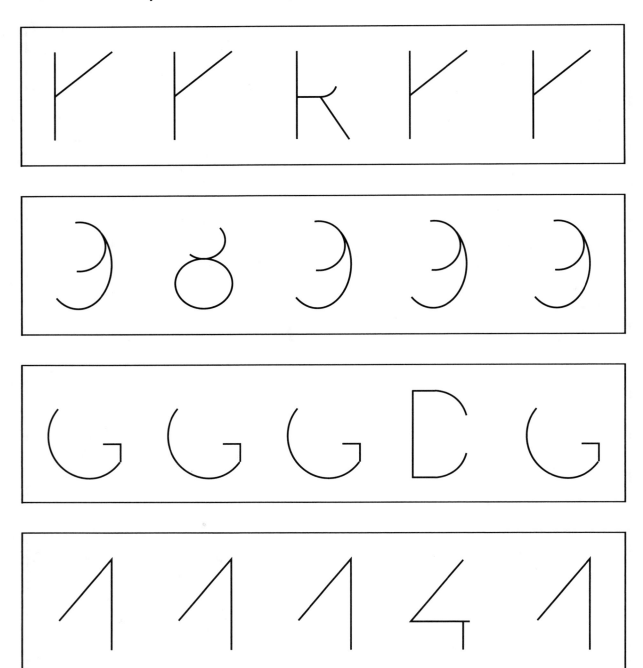

LESSON 1 Visual Discrimination

Circle the shape that is different.

| ㅏ Z Z Z Z |

| Ɛ Ɛ 5 Ɛ Ɛ |

| Z Z 2 Z Z |

| P P P P O |

LESSON 1 Visual Discrimination

10

Circle the shape that is the same.

K | K ▷ ⱼ Z |

K | K Y ⱼ Z |

D | P O G D |

5 | 8 ⊃ ⊂ O |

LESSON 1 Visual Discrimination

Circle the shape that is the same.

LESSON 1 Visual Discrimination

12

Match the shapes.

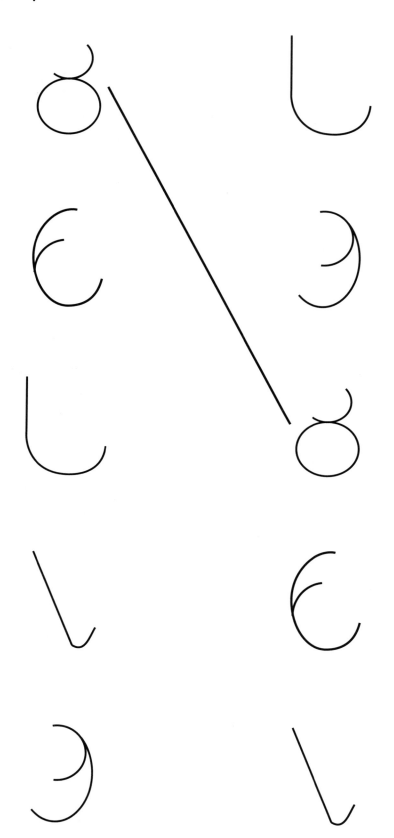

LESSON 1 Visual Discrimination

13

Match the shapes.

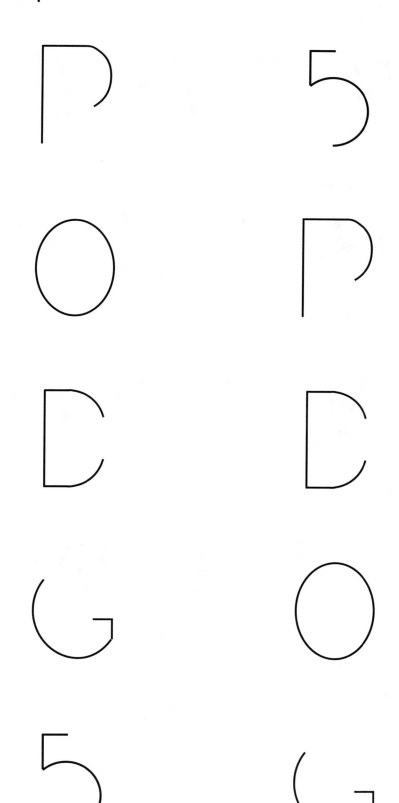

LESSON 2 The Alphabet

THE ALPHABET

A B C D E F
G H I J K L
M N O P Q R
S T U V W X
Y Z

LESSON 2 The Alphabet

Circle the letter that is the same.

t	d	l	(t)	i
A	V	O	H	(A)
g	p	q	c	(g)
t	d	l	t	i
A	V	O	H	A
g	p	q	c	g
M	N	M	W	V
b	b	h	k	p
r	q	r	k	f
H	H	L	I	T
X	Y	J	Z	X
e	c	o	e	a
P	B	D	P	Q
Z	S	R	Z	V

LESSON 2 The Alphabet

Circle the letter that is the same.

j	y	g	q	j
f	t	f	h	e
l	i	t	l	k
D	Q	O	P	D
n	n	m	w	u
I	L	T	J	I
S	Z	X	G	S
V	V	W	U	N
q	p	g	q	y
w	m	n	v	w
c	e	o	a	c
k	f	k	l	h
y	g	j	q	y
u	w	u	v	n
o	c	q	e	o

LESSON 2 The Alphabet

Trace the letter.

A A A A A A A A

Copy the letter.

A

Trace the letter.

B B B B B B B B

Copy the letter.

B

LESSON 2 The Alphabet

Trace the letter.

C C C C C C C C

Copy the letter.

C

Trace the letter.

D D D D D D D D

Copy the letter.

D

LESSON 2 The Alphabet

Trace the letter.

E E E E E E E

Copy the letter.

E

Trace the letter.

F F F F F F F

Copy the letter.

F

LESSON 2 The Alphabet

Trace the letter.

Copy the letter.

Trace the letter.

Copy the letter.

LESSON 2 The Alphabet

Trace the letter.

Copy the letter.

Trace the letter.

Copy the letter.

LESSON 2 The Alphabet

Trace the letter.

K K K K K K K

Copy the letter.

K

Trace the letter.

L L L L L L L

Copy the letter.

L

LESSON 2 The Alphabet

23

Trace the letter.

Copy the letter.

Trace the letter.

Copy the letter.

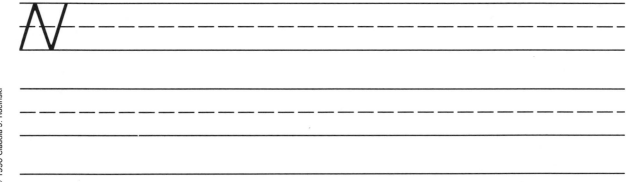

LESSON 2 The Alphabet

Trace the letter.

O O O O O O O O

Copy the letter.

O

Trace the letter.

P P P P P P P P

Copy the letter.

P

LESSON 2 The Alphabet

25

Trace the letter.

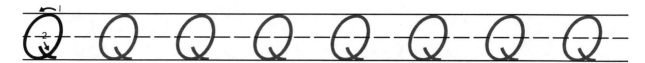

Copy the letter.

Trace the letter.

Copy the letter.

LESSON 2 The Alphabet

Trace the letter.

S S S S S S S S

Copy the letter.

S

Trace the letter.

T T T T T T T T

Copy the letter.

T

LESSON 2 The Alphabet 27

Trace the letter.

Copy the letter.

Trace the letter.

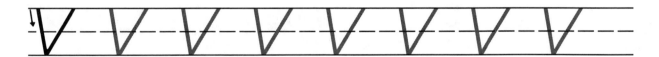

Copy the letter.

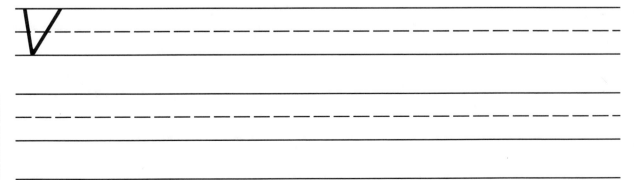

LESSON 2 The Alphabet

Trace the letter.

Copy the letter.

Trace the letter.

Copy the letter.

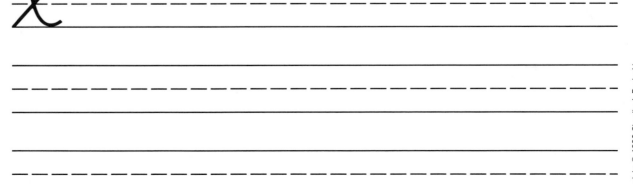

LESSON 2 The Alphabet

Trace the letter.

Y Y Y Y Y Y Y Y Y

Copy the letter.

Y

Trace the letter.

Z Z Z Z Z Z Z Z Z

Copy the letter.

Z

LESSON 2 The Alphabet

CAPITAL LETTER	small letter
A	a
B	b
C	c
D	d
E	e
F	f
G	g
H	h
I	i
J	j
K	k
L	l
M	m
N	n
O	o
P	p
Q	q
R	r
S	s
T	t
U	u
V	v
W	w
X	x
Y	y
Z	z

LESSON 2 The Alphabet

THE ALPHABET

a b c d e f

g h i j k l

m n o p q r

s t u v w x

y z

LESSON 2 The Alphabet

Trace the letter.

a a a a a a a a

Copy the letter.

a

Trace the letter.

b b b b b b b b

Copy the letter.

b

LESSON 2 The Alphabet

Trace the letter.

C C C C C C C C

Copy the letter.

C

Trace the letter.

d d d d d d d d

Copy the letter.

d

LESSON 2 The Alphabet

Trace the letter.

e e e e e e e e

Copy the letter.

e

Trace the letter.

f f f f f f f f

Copy the letter.

f

LESSON 2 The Alphabet

Trace the letter.

Copy the letter.

Trace the letter.

Copy the letter.

LESSON 2 The Alphabet

Trace the letter.

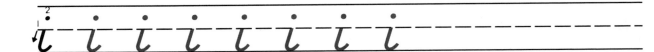

Copy the letter.

Trace the letter.

Copy the letter.

LESSON 2 The Alphabet

Trace the letter.

Copy the letter.

Trace the letter.

Copy the letter.

LESSON 2 The Alphabet

Trace the letter.

m m m m m m m m

Copy the letter.

m

Trace the letter.

n n n n n n n

Copy the letter.

n

LESSON 2 The Alphabet

Trace the letter.

O O O O O O O O

Copy the letter.

O

Trace the letter.

p p p p p p p p

Copy the letter.

p

LESSON 2 The Alphabet

Trace the letter.

q q q q q q q q q

Copy the letter.

q

Trace the letter.

r r r r r r r r

Copy the letter.

r

LESSON 2 The Alphabet

Trace the letter.

s s s s s s s

Copy the letter.

s

Trace the letter.

t t t t t t t

Copy the letter.

t

LESSON 2 The Alphabet

Trace the letter.

𝓤 𝓤 𝓤 𝓤 𝓤 𝓤 𝓤 𝓤

Copy the letter.

𝓤

Trace the letter.

𝓥 𝓥 𝓥 𝓥 𝓥 𝓥 𝓥 𝓥

Copy the letter.

𝓥

LESSON 2 The Alphabet

Trace the letter.

w w w w w w w w

Copy the letter.

w

Trace the letter.

x x x x x x x x

Copy the letter.

x

LESSON 2 The Alphabet

Trace the letter.

y y y y y y y y y

Copy the letter.

y

Trace the letter.

z z z z z z z z

Copy the letter.

z

LESSON 2 The Alphabet

45

Match the letters.

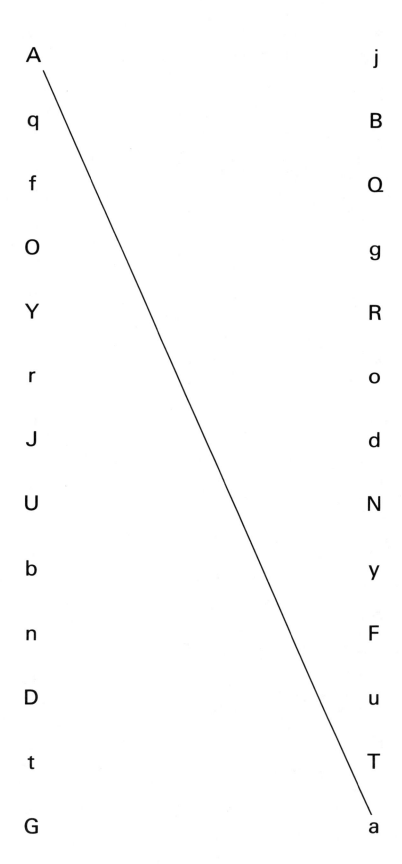

A	j
q	B
f	Q
O	g
Y	R
r	o
J	d
U	N
b	y
n	F
D	u
t	T
G	a

LESSON 2 The Alphabet

Match the letters.

Z	M
c	E
I	X
S	h
v	V
x	w
W	p
P	i
m	z
e	k
H	C
K	L
I	s

LESSON 2 The Alphabet

Circle the capital letter.

| b | d | (D) | t | o | a |

b	d	D	t	o	a
s	x	r	q	f	G
o	U	y	h	u	k
c	m	t	w	B	l
X	u	i	j	x	a
m	q	a	h	p	A
t	P	s	q	p	f
h	m	u	y	Y	x
j	k	b	J	c	o
C	o	a	c	g	n

LESSON 2 The Alphabet

Circle the capital letter.

f	k	r	F	h	g
t	H	k	g	m	h
z	s	r	Z	c	e
p	e	c	q	o	E
h	k	I	i	l	t
K	h	k	w	x	v
O	o	a	p	q	u
u	x	m	s	S	x
v	u	V	y	w	a
j	L	k	l	i	h
M	m	n	k	f	g

LESSON 2 The Alphabet

Circle the capital letters.

| a | Ⓞ | Ⓐ | e | Ⓤ | Ⓟ |

a	O	A	e	U	P
B	d	T	I	I	x
J	G	w	j	L	H
t	d	l	T	y	X
z	q	R	f	K	c
D	O	C	e	S	V
m	N	E	H	Y	F

LESSON 2 The Alphabet

Circle the capital letters.

W	x	n	J	q	z
f	r	D	B	p	z
V	W	K	t	d	J
a	E	o	u	v	X
D	O	C	L	Q	e
G	q	h	M	B	d
e	o	R	n	I	l
C	O	o	e	v	X
J	l	B	P	L	b

LESSON 2 The Alphabet

Circle the small letter.

| A | M | P | B | ⓑ | D |

A	M	P	B	b	D
P	k	H	K	L	W
M	W	X	m	N	O
A	c	C	Y	D	Q
r	T	R	S	B	V
U	S	J	g	G	Q
F	P	w	V	U	W
F	i	I	L	T	K
A	O	P	D	B	d

LESSON 2 The Alphabet

Circle the small letter.

s	S	X	Z	H	J
T	N	e	F	E	O
V	H	N	K	n	M
F	B	L	V	U	v
o	O	A	Q	G	B
B	p	P	G	C	D
S	H	I	x	X	Z
Q	B	b	D	P	T
L	H	I	T	I	K
N	Q	M	L	z	V
j	J	G	S	V	U

LESSON 2 The Alphabet

Circle the small letters.

F	ⓠ	N	ⓞ	ⓔ	G

F	q	N	o	e	G
x	s	Y	B	D	f
l	L	i	k	a	D
Y	w	x	h	N	m
r	v	c	J	D	A
N	f	S	T	h	p
L	i	l	d	t	Y

LESSON 2 The Alphabet

Circle the small letters.

i	j	U	V	u	w
C	q	Q	E	g	K
e	o	F	V	w	N
h	L	t	r	g	H
P	Q	b	d	N	E
s	X	Z	C	o	P
a	d	z	e	r	K
F	t	E	G	d	O
V	x	y	Z	S	n

LESSON 2 The Alphabet

Cross out the letter that does not belong.

A	B	~~X~~	C	D	E
P	Q	R	S	~~X~~	T
M	~~X~~	N	O	P	Q

A	B	D	C	D	E
P	Q	R	S	U	T
M	O	N	O	P	Q
J	L	K	L	M	N
C	D	E	G	F	G
H	J	I	J	K	L

LESSON 2 The Alphabet

Cross out the letter that does not belong.

G	H	J	I	J	K
D	F	E	F	G	H
Q	R	V	S	T	U
B	C	D	E	F	H
I	J	K	L	N	M
R	S	T	V	U	V
O	Q	P	Q	R	S
E	F	G	H	I	K
M	V	N	O	P	Q

LESSON 2 The Alphabet

Cross out the letter that does not belong.

a	b	d	c	d	e
p	q	r	s	u	t
m	o	n	o	p	q
f	h	g	h	i	j
v	w	x	w	y	z
j	k	l	m	o	n
b	c	d	f	e	f
s	t	v	u	v	w
k	l	n	m	n	o

LESSON 2 The Alphabet

Cross out the letter that does not belong.

c	d	e	f	g	i
o	q	p	q	r	s
i	k	j	k	l	m
t	u	v	w	y	x
e	g	f	g	h	i
u	v	w	x	y	x
g	h	j	i	j	k
p	r	s	t	u	v
v	w	y	x	y	z

LESSON 2 The Alphabet

Cross out the letter that does not belong.

A	b	D	c	D	E
I	M	N	p	O	p
H	J	i	j	k	L
p	q	O	R	s	T
d	f	E	F	g	h
U	w	V	W	x	y
K	L	m	n	O	Q
E	f	I	G	H	I
c	d	E	F	g	i

LESSON 2 The Alphabet

Cross out the letter that does not belong.

L	m	N	Q	o	p
T	V	u	v	w	X
d	E	F	I	g	H
O	p	q	R	T	s
V	w	x	y	X	z
n	p	o	P	Q	R
B	C	e	D	E	f
J	L	K	l	m	n
r	T	s	t	U	V
U	V	W	x	y	x

LESSON 2 The Alphabet

Write the missing letters.

A   B   C   D   ___   F

G   ___   I   ___   K   ___

M   ___   ___   P   ___   R

___   T   ___   ___   W   X

___   Z

Write the missing letters.

a   b   ___   d   e   ___

g   h   ___   j   k   ___

___   ___   o   p   ___   ___

s   t   ___   v   w   ___

y   ___

LESSON 2 The Alphabet

Write the alphabet.

A   *B*   ___   ___   ___   ___

___   ___   ___   ___   ___   ___

___   ___   ___   ___   ___   ___

___   ___   ___   ___   ___   ___

___   ___

Write the alphabet.

a   *b*   ___   ___   ___   ___

___   ___   ___   ___   ___   ___

___   ___   ___   ___   ___   ___

___   ___   ___   ___   ___   ___

___   ___

LESSON 3 Name _____ **63**

Jane Marie Lund

Chang Lee

LESSON 3 Name

64

Circle the word that is the same.

| NAME | NOSE | MANE | (NAME) | NONE |

NAME	NOSE	MANE	NAME	NONE
FIRST	FISH	FIST	FIVE	FIRST
MIDDLE	MIDDLE	MIDLAND	MEDAL	MODAL
LAST	LASH	LASS	LAST	LATCH
Name	Nave	Man	Nape	Name
First	Fifth	First	Fit	Firm
Middle	Mediate	Midst	Mild	Middle
Last	Land	Lane	Lest	Last

Match the words.

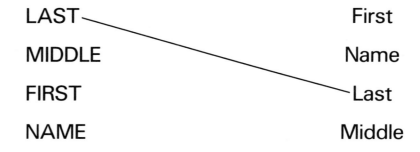

LESSON 3 Name

Copy your name.

NAME _____

FIRST NAME _____

MIDDLE NAME _____

LAST NAME _____

FIRST NAME _____

FIRST NAME _____

FIRST NAME _____

FIRST NAME _____

FIRST NAME _____

MIDDLE NAME _____

MIDDLE NAME _____

MIDDLE NAME _____

MIDDLE NAME _____

MIDDLE NAME _____

LAST NAME _____

LAST NAME _____

LAST NAME _____

LAST NAME _____

LAST NAME _____

LESSON 3 Name

Copy your name.

NAME _____

FIRST _____

MIDDLE _____

LAST _____

First _____

FIRST _____

First _____

First _____

FIRST _____

MIDDLE _____

MIDDLE _____

Middle _____

MIDDLE _____

Middle _____

Last _____

LAST _____

LAST _____

Last _____

Last _____

LESSON 3 Name

Copy your name.

Last _____

FIRST _____

Middle _____

LAST _____

First _____

Last _____

LAST _____

First _____

MIDDLE _____

FIRST _____

Middle _____

NAME _____

Name _____

NAME _____

Name _____

LESSON 3 Name

Copy your name.

NAME _____
　　　　　First

NAME _____
　　　　　First

NAME _____
　　　　　FIRST

NAME _____
　　　　　First

NAME _____
　　　　　FIRST

NAME _____
　　　　　First　　　　　　Middle

NAME _____
　　　　　FIRST　　　　　　MIDDLE

NAME _____
　　　　　First　　　　　　Middle

Name _____
　　　　　First　　　　　　Middle

NAME _____
　　　　　FIRST　　　　　　MIDDLE

LESSON 3 Name

Copy your name.

NAME _____
              First   Middle   Last

NAME _____
              FIRST   MIDDLE   LAST

Name _____
              First   Middle   Last

NAME _____
              FIRST   MIDDLE   LAST

Name _____
              First   Middle   Last

NAME _____
              Last   First   Middle

NAME _____
              LAST   FIRST   MIDDLE

Name _____
              Last   First   Middle

NAME _____
              Last   First   Middle

NAME _____
              LAST   FIRST   MIDDLE

LESSON 3 Name

Middle Initial = MI

Copy.

Middle Initial _____

Middle Initial _____

Middle Initial _____

MI _____

MI _____

MI _____

Write.

Name _____
          Last   First   MI

NAME _____
          LAST   FIRST   MI

Name _____
          First   MI   Last

NAME _____
          FIRST   MI   LAST

LESSON 3 Name

71

Write your name.

NAME _____
              First   Middle   Last

NAME _____
              FIRST   MIDDLE   LAST

Name _____
              Last   First   Middle

Name _____
              First   Middle   Last

NAME _____
              LAST   FIRST   MIDDLE

NAME _____

Name _____

Name _____

NAME _____

Name _____

It's Your Cue

My name is _____

LESSON 3 Name

72

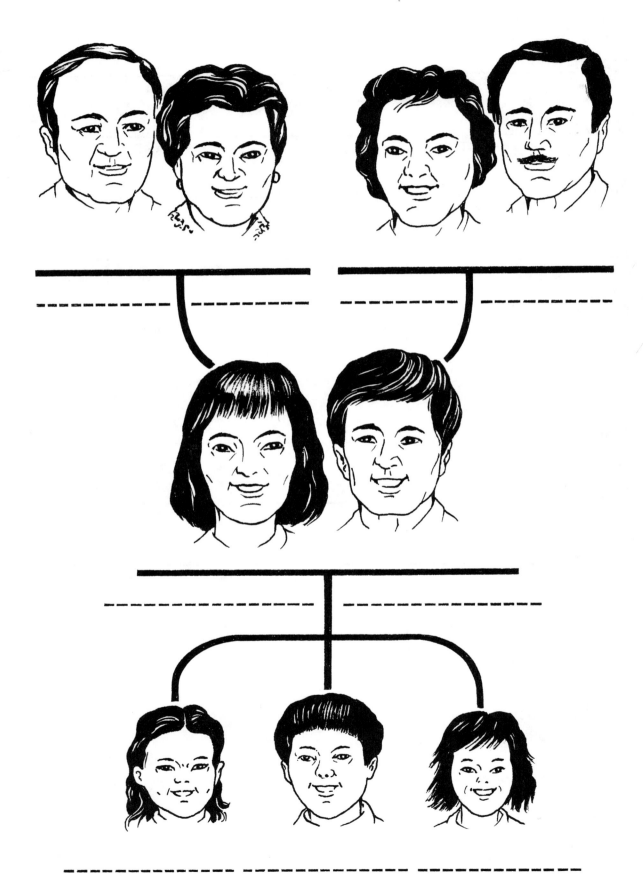

LESSON 3 Name 73

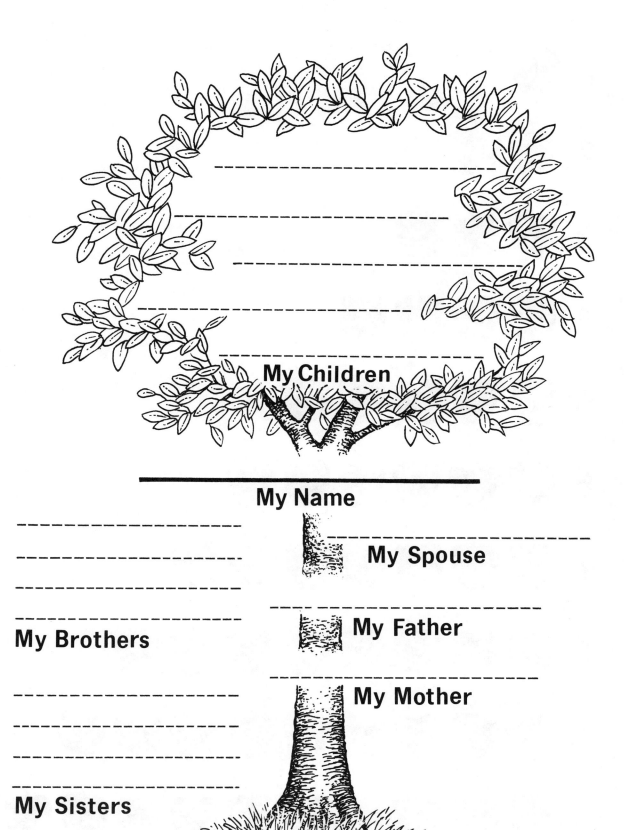

LESSON 4 Numbers 1–10

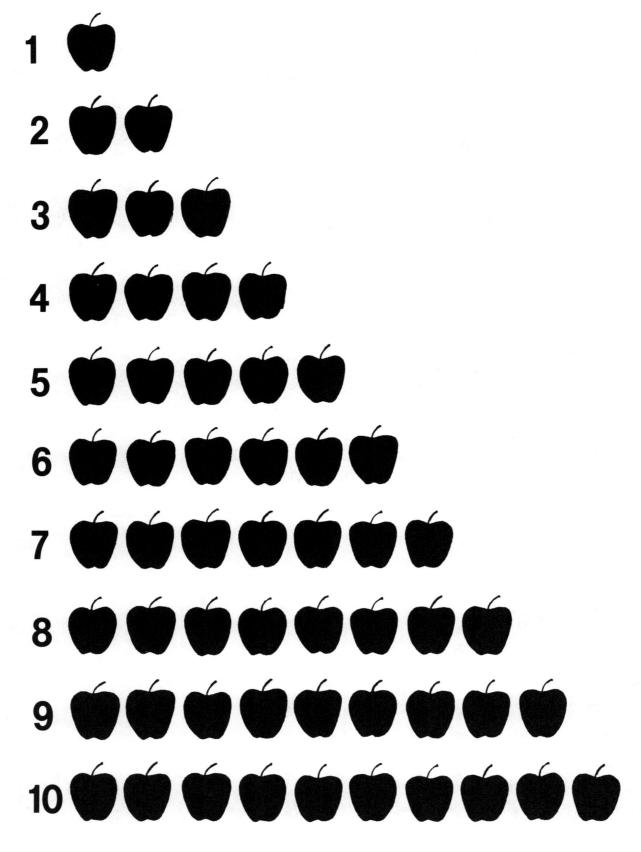

LESSON 4 Numbers 1–10

1 2 3 4 5

6 7 8 9 10

LESSON 4 Numbers 1–10

76

Circle the number that is the same.

3	6	9	③	2
8	9	⑧	0	6
1	10	7	2	①

3	6	9	3	2
8	9	8	0	6
1	10	7	2	1
5	5	4	7	6
9	6	9	2	10
2	3	7	6	2
10	1	0	10	9
7	7	4	1	6
6	9	6	3	7
4	1	7	5	4

LESSON 4 Numbers 1–10

77

Match the number with the picture.

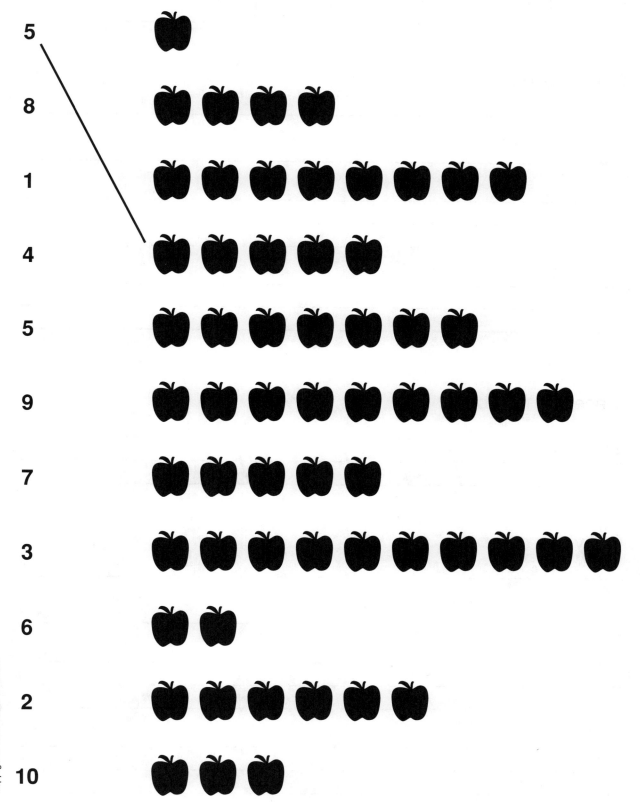

LESSON 4 Numbers 1–10

Trace the number.

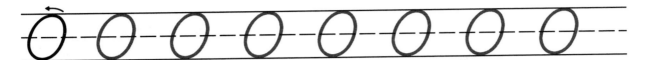

Copy the number.

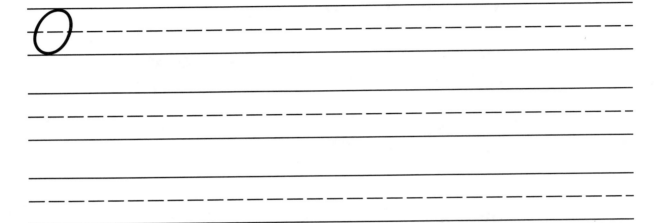

Trace the number.

Copy the number.

LESSON 4 Numbers 1–10

Trace the number.

2 2 2 2 2 2 2 2

Copy the number.

2

Trace the number.

3 3 3 3 3 3 3 3

Copy the number.

3

LESSON 4 Numbers 1–10

Trace the number.

4 4 4 4 4 4 4 4

Copy the number.

4

Trace the number.

5 5 5 5 5 5 5 5

Copy the number.

5

LESSON 4 Numbers 1–10

Trace the number.

6 6 6 6 6 6 6 6

Copy the number.

6

Trace the number.

7 7 7 7 7 7 7 7

Copy the number.

7

LESSON 4 Numbers 1–10

Trace the number.

$8\ 8\ 8\ 8\ 8\ 8\ 8\ 8$

Copy the number.

8

Trace the number.

$9\ 9\ 9\ 9\ 9\ 9\ 9\ 9$

Copy the number.

9

LESSON 4 Numbers 1–10 **83**

1	*2*	*3*	*4*	*5*
one	two	three	four	five
6	*7*	*8*	*9*	*10*
six	seven	eight	nine	ten

LESSON 4 Numbers 1–10

Circle the word that is the same as the number.

| 3 | four | two | (three) | ten |

3	four	two	three	ten
10	one	nine	ten	two
7	eleven	seven	six	one
2	two	ten	three	four
4	fourteen	five	fifteen	four
1	ten	one	eleven	seven
5	four	fifteen	five	fifty
6	seven	six	sixteen	sixty
8	eighteen	eighty	nine	eight
9	eight	nineteen	ninety	nine

LESSON 4 Numbers 1–10

85

Match the number and the word.

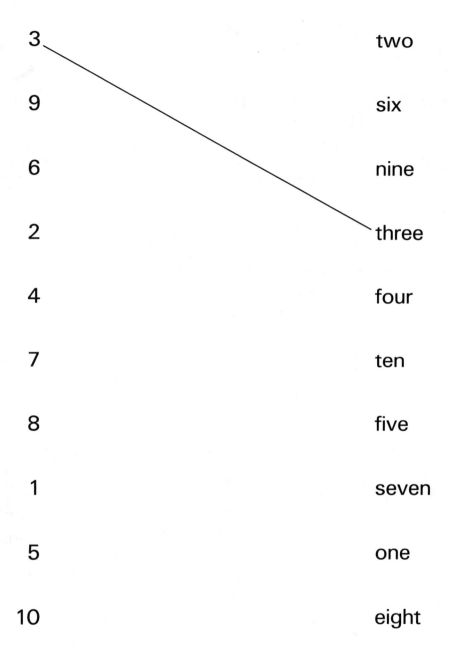

LESSON 4 Numbers 1–10

Copy.

1
one

one

2
two

two

3
three

three

4
four

four

5
five

five

6
six

six

LESSON 4 Numbers 1–10

Copy.

7
seven

seven

8
eight

eight

9
nine

nine

10
ten

ten

LESSON 4 Numbers 1–10

Write the word.

1	6	3
one	six	three
1	6	3
___	___	___
4	2	9
___	___	___
10	1	8
___	___	___
5	7	2
___	___	___

LESSON 4 Numbers 1–10 # 89

Write the word.

10	4	7
_____	_____	_____
3	8	1
_____	_____	_____
6	5	2
_____	_____	_____
9	10	4
_____	_____	_____
5	7	8
_____	_____	_____

LESSON 4 Numbers 1–10

It's Your Cue

Write the number you hear.

___ ___ ___ ___ ___ ___ ___ ___ ___ ___ ___ ___

A _____

B _____

C _____

D _____

E _____

F _____

G _____

H _____

I _____

J _____

LESSON 5 Telephone Number

LESSON 5 Telephone Number

Circle the word that is the same.

| Telephone | Telephoto Television (Telephone) Telegraph |

Telephone	Telephoto	Television	Telephone	Telegraph
Number	Number	Numb	Numeral	Nubbin
AREA	ARENA	ARE	ARIA	AREA
Code	Cod	Coke	Code	Cob

Match the words.

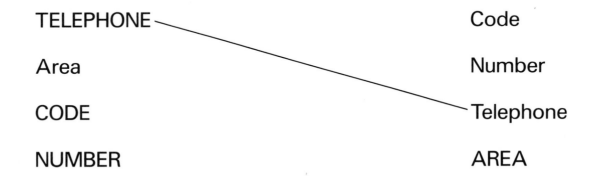

TELEPHONE — Code

Area — Number

CODE — Telephone

NUMBER — AREA

LESSON 5 Telephone Number

Copy.

Area Code (___ ___ ___)

AREA CODE (___ ___ ___)

Area Code (___ ___ ___)

Telephone Number (___ ___ ___) ___ ___ ___ - ___ ___ ___

TELEPHONE NUMBER (___ ___ ___) ___ ___ ___ - ___ ___ ___

Telephone (_____) _____ - _____

TELEPHONE (_____) _____ - _____

Telephone Number _____

Telephone _____
(Area Code)

_____
(Area Code)   Telephone

(_____)
_____
              Telephone

_____
              Telephone

It's Your Cue

My telephone number is _____

LESSON 6 Social Security Number

LESSON 6 Social Security Number

Circle the word that is the same.

| SOCIAL | SOCIETY | SOLDIER | SABLE | (SOCIAL) |

SOCIAL	SOCIETY	SOLDIER	SABLE	SOCIAL
Security	Securely	Security	Secondary	Secretary
NUMBER	NUMERAL	NUMB	NUMERATE	NUMBER

Match the words.

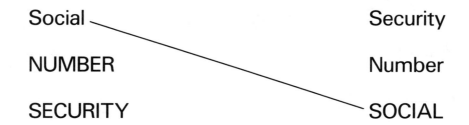

LESSON 6 Social Security Number

Copy.

SOCIAL SECURITY NUMBER ___ ___ ___ – ___ ___ – ___ ___ ___ ___

Social Security Number ___ ___ ___ – ___ ___ – ___ ___ ___ ___

Social Security Number ___ ___ ___ – ___ ___ – ___ ___ ___ ___

SOCIAL SECURITY NUMBER ___ ___ ___ – ___ ___ – ___ ___ ___ ___

Social Security Number ___ ___ ___ – ___ ___ – ___ ___ ___ ___

SOCIAL SECURITY NUMBER ☐ ☐ ☐ – ☐ ☐ – ☐ ☐ ☐ ☐

Social Security Number ☐ ☐ ☐ – ☐ ☐ – ☐ ☐ ☐ ☐

SOCIAL SECURITY NUMBER ☐ ☐ ☐ – ☐ ☐ – ☐ ☐ ☐ ☐

Social Security Number _____ – _____ – _____

SOCIAL SECURITY NUMBER _____ – _____ – _____

Social Security Number _____

Social Security Number _____

Social Security Number _____

Social Security Number _____

It's Your Cue

My Social Security number is _____

CHECKUP 1

NAME _____
         Last   First   MI

TELEPHONE NUMBER (_____) _____

SOCIAL SECURITY NUMBER _____ – _____ – _____

LESSON 7 Numbers 11–19

11 12 13

14 15 16

17 18 19

LESSON 7 Numbers 11–19

Circle the number that is the same.

| 12 | 2 | 21 | 13 | ⟨12⟩ | 22 |

12	2	21	13	12	22
15	51	15	14	5	19
16	19	61	16	9	18
18	8	18	81	19	6
11	10	21	1	17	11
17	11	17	14	18	7
13	31	13	16	19	10
19	18	10	19	91	16
14	11	7	41	14	4

LESSON 7 Numbers 11–19

11	*12*	*13*
eleven	twelve	thirteen
14	*15*	*16*
fourteen	fifteen	sixteen
17	*18*	*19*
seventeen	eighteen	nineteen

LESSON 7 Numbers 11–19

Circle the word that is the same as the number.

| 1 | (one) | four | ten | eleven |

1	one	four	ten	eleven
10	ten	eight	nine	twelve
14	twenty	fourteen	eighteen	fifteen
3	two	thirteen	eight	three
7	seventeen	one	seven	eleven
13	thirty	twelve	three	thirteen
5	five	fifteen	four	fifty
19	ninety	nineteen	nine	eighteen
4	fourteen	five	four	forty
8	nine	six	eighteen	eight

LESSON 7 Numbers 11–19

Match the number to the word.

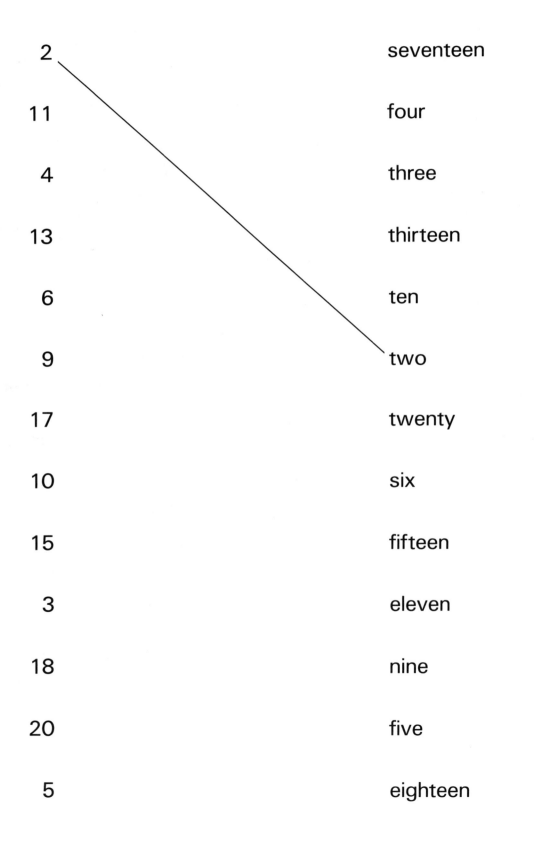

LESSON 7 Numbers 11–19

Copy.

11
eleven

eleven

12
twelve

twelve

13
thirteen

thirteen

14
fourteen

fourteen

LESSON 7 Numbers 11–19

Copy.

15
fifteen

fifteen

16
sixteen

sixteen

17
seventeen

seventeen

18
eighteen

eighteen

Copy.

19
nineteen

nineteen

LESSON 7 Numbers 11–19

Write the missing letters.

12   t ___ e l v e

19   n i n e t ___ ___ n

14   f ___ ___ r t e e n

16   s i ___ t e e n

18   ___ ___ g h t e e n

15   f i ___ t e e n

11   ___ ___ e v e n

17   s e ___ e n t e e n

13   ___ ___ i r t e e n

LESSON 7 Numbers 11–19

Write the missing numbers and words.

11
eleven

_____

13
thirteen

_____

15
fifteen

16
sixteen

LESSON 7 Numbers 11–19

Write the words.

11
eleven

15
fifteen

19

13

12

14

17

11

16

18

LESSON 7 Numbers 11–19

Write the words.

19	17
___	___
12	15
___	___
17	18
___	___
13	11
___	___
14	16
___	___

LESSON 8 Numbers 20–100

20 21 22 23 24 25 26 27 28 29

30 31 32 33 34 35 36 37 38 39

40 41 42 43 44 45 46 47 48 49

50 51 52 53 54 55 56 57 58 59

60 61 62 63 64 65 66 67 68 69

70 71 72 73 74 75 76 77 78 79

80 81 82 83 84 85 86 87 88 89

90 91 92 93 94 95 96 97 98 99

100

LESSON 8 Numbers 20–100

111

Circle the number that is the same.

| 20 | ⬭20⬭ | 2 | 12 | 13 | 29 |

20	20	2	12	13	29
51	15	41	57	51	55
73	13	73	37	17	72
88	80	86	89	68	88
36	30	86	36	63	39
65	64	65	56	95	35
42	42	41	12	43	24
94	64	91	84	95	94
47	17	74	47	41	44
68	88	98	86	68	28
100	109	101	106	108	100

LESSON 8 Numbers 20–100

112

Write the missing numbers.

| 20 | 21 | 22 | ___ | 24 | 25 | 26 | 27 | 28 |

| 29 | ___ | 31 | 32 | 33 | 34 | 35 | 36 | ___ |

| 38 | 39 | 40 | ___ | 42 | 43 | ___ | 45 | 46 |

| 47 | ___ | 49 | 50 | 51 | ___ | 53 | 54 | ___ |

| 56 | 57 | 58 | ___ | ___ | 61 | 62 | 63 | 64 |

| ___ | ___ | 67 | 68 | 69 | 70 | ___ | ___ | 73 |

| 74 | 75 | 76 | ___ | 78 | 79 | ___ | 81 | 82 |

| ___ | 84 | ___ | 86 | ___ | 88 | ___ | ___ | ___ |

| 92 | 93 | ___ | ___ | ___ | 97 | ___ | ___ | ___ |

LESSON 8 Numbers 20–100

20 twenty	21 twenty-one	22 twenty-two	23 twenty-three	24 twenty-four
25 twenty-five	26 twenty-six	27 twenty-seven	28 twenty-eight	29 twenty-nine
30 thirty	31 thirty-one	32 thirty-two	33 thirty-three	34 thirty-four
35 thirty-five	36 thirty-six	37 thirty-seven	38 thirty-eight	39 thirty-nine
40 forty	41 forty-one	42 forty-two	43 forty-three	44 forty-four
45 forty-five	46 forty-six	47 forty-seven	48 forty-eight	49 forty-nine

LESSON 8 Numbers 20–100

50	51	52	53	54
fifty	fifty-one	fifty-two	fifty-three	fifty-four

55	56	57	58	59
fifty-five	fifty-six	fifty-seven	fifty-eight	fifty-nine

60	61	62	63	64
sixty	sixty-one	sixty-two	sixty-three	sixty-four

65	66	67	68	69
sixty-five	sixty-six	sixty-seven	sixty-eight	sixty-nine

70	71	72	73	74
seventy	seventy-one	seventy-two	seventy-three	seventy-four

75	76	77	78	79
seventy-five	seventy-six	seventy-seven	seventy-eight	seventy-nine

LESSON 8 Numbers 20–100

80 eighty
81 eighty-one
82 eighty-two
83 eighty-three
84 eighty-four

85 eighty-five
86 eighty-six
87 eighty-seven
88 eighty-eight
89 eighty-nine

90 ninety
91 ninety-one
92 ninety-two
93 ninety-three
94 ninety-four

95 ninety-five
96 ninety-six
97 ninety-seven
98 ninety-eight
99 ninety-nine

100 one hundred

LESSON 8 Numbers 20–100

Match the number with the word.

66	sixty-four
85	twenty-two
71	ninety-nine
22	ninety-three
58	fifty-eight
93	one hundred
37	eighty-five
64	seventy-one
49	twenty
100	sixty-six
55	thirty-seven
99	fifty-five
20	forty-nine

LESSON 8 Numbers 20–100

Write the missing numbers and words.

20   21   22   23
twenty   twenty-one   twenty-two   twenty-three

24   26   27
twenty-four _____   twenty-six   twenty-seven

             29   31
_____   twenty-nine   _____   thirty-one

32   34   35
thirty-two   _____   thirty-four   thirty-five

36   38
thirty-six   _____   thirty-eight _____

LESSON 8 Numbers 20–100 **118**

Write the missing numbers and words.

_____   _____   42   43
                        forty-two   forty-three

44   _____   46   47
forty-four   forty-six   forty-seven

48   49   50   51
forty-eight   forty-nine   fifty   fifty-one

_____   53   _____   _____
             fifty-three

56   _____   58   _____
fifty-six   fifty-eight

LESSON 8 Numbers 20–100

Write the missing numbers and words.

_____   **61**   **62**   **63**
            sixty-one   sixty-two   sixty-three

       65   **67**
_____   sixty-five   _____   sixty-seven

       69   **70**   **71**
_____   sixty-nine   seventy   seventy-one

72   **73**   **74**
seventy-two   seventy-three   seventy-four   _____

                  78
_____   _____   seventy-eight   _____

LESSON 8 Numbers 20–100

Write the missing numbers and words.

80   81   _____   83
eighty   eighty-one   _____   eighty-three

84   _____   86   87
eighty-four   _____   eighty-six   eighty-seven

_____   89   _____   _____
_____   eighty-nine   _____   _____

92   _____   _____   95
ninety-two   _____   _____   ninety-five

_____   97   98   _____
_____   ninety-seven   ninety-eight   _____

_____

LESSON 9 Address—Number and Street

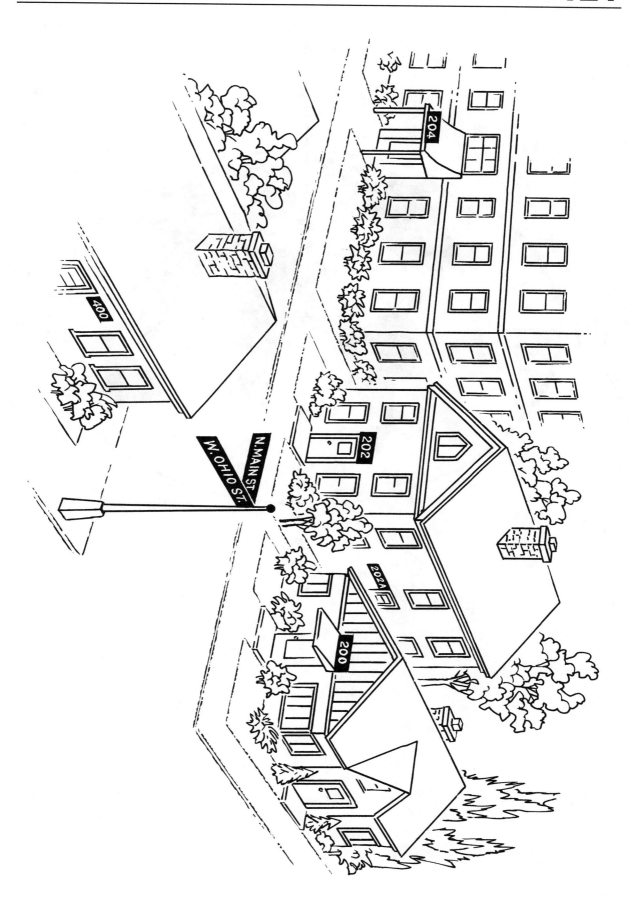

LESSON 9 Address—Number and Street

122

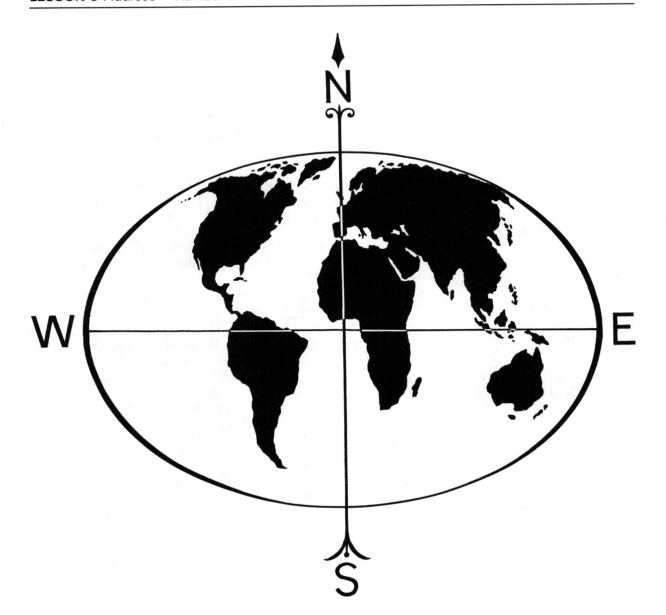

LESSON 9 Address—Number and Street

Circle the word that is the same.

| Address | Added | Adduce | (Address) | Advice |

Address	Added	Adduce	Address	Advice
NUMBER	NUMB	NURSE	NUTTY	NUMBER
Street	Stream	Street	Stretch	Strength
ADDRESS	ADULT	ADDEND	ADJUST	ADDRESS
Number	Muster	Number	Mumble	Nurture
STREET	STREAK	STRESS	STREET	STRIKE

Match the words.

NUMBER   Street

Address   Number

STREET   ADDRESS

LESSON 9 Address—Number and Street

Number   =   No.

Street   =   St.

Match the words.

ADDRESS   St.

No.   Address

Street   NUMBER

LESSON 9 Address—Number and Street

Copy.

North   N.   *N.* __ __ __ __ __ __

South   S.   *S.* __ __ __ __ __ __

East   E.   *E.* __ __ __ __ __ __

West   W.   *W.* __ __ __ __ __ __

LESSON 9 Address—Number and Street

Copy.

Number _____

Number _____

NUMBER _____

Number _____

NUMBER _____

Number _____

Street _____

STREET _____

Street _____

STREET _____

Street _____

Street _____

LESSON 9 Address—Number and Street

Copy.

ADDRESS _____
                    Number   Street

ADDRESS _____
                    Number   Street

Address _____
                    Number   Street

ADDRESS _____
                    NUMBER   STREET

Address _____
                    Number   Street

ADDRESS _____
                    NUMBER   STREET

Address _____
                    Number   Street

ADDRESS _____
                    NUMBER   STREET

Address _____
                    Number   Street

LESSON 9 Address—Number and Street

Write.

Address _____
                No.   St.

ADDRESS _____
                NO.   ST.

ADDRESS _____
                No.   St.

Address _____
                No.   St.

Address _____
                No.   St.

ADDRESS _____
                NO.   ST.

ADDRESS _____
                No.   St.

Address _____
                No.   St.

ADDRESS _____
                NO.   ST.

It's Your Cue

My address is _____.

WORD SEARCH 1

Can you find and circle these words?

name	area
address	code
street	number

---

b	n	a	m	e	g	x	a	u
g	u	d	t	a	r	e	a	h
i	m	d	p	v	o	c	n	q
a	b	r	x	c	g	o	u	m
j	e	e	f	h	k	d	b	t
q	r	s	t	r	e	e	t	l
x	c	s	x	f	n	p	k	y

LESSON 10 Address—City, State, and Zip Code

130

LESSON 10 Address—City, State, and Zip Code

131

Circle the word that is the same.

| City | Civil | Cite | (City) | Cent |

City	Civil	Cite	City	Cent
State	Stay	Straw	Start	State
Zip Code	Zipper	Cod	Zip Code	Zinc

Match the words.

CITY   State

Zip Code   City

STATE   ZIP CODE

LESSON 10 Address—City, State, and Zip Code

Copy.

CITY _____

CITY _____

CITY _____

CITY _____

STATE _____

STATE _____

STATE _____

STATE _____

ZIP CODE _____

ZIP CODE _____

ZIP CODE _____

ZIP CODE _____

LESSON 10 Address—City, State, and Zip Code

Write.

City _____

ZIP CODE _____

State _____

STATE _____

Zip Code _____

CITY _____

ZIP CODE _____

State _____

City _____

CITY _____

STATE _____

Zip Code _____

LESSON 10 Address—City, State, and Zip Code

134

Write.

City｜State｜Zip Code

CITY｜STATE｜ZIP CODE

City｜State｜Zip Code

City｜State｜Zip Code

CITY｜STATE｜ZIP CODE

City｜State｜Zip Code

City｜State｜Zip Code

CITY｜STATE｜ZIP CODE

City｜State｜Zip Code

CITY｜STATE｜ZIP CODE

LESSON 10 Address—City, State, and Zip Code

Write.

ADDRESS _____
                Number   Street

                 _____
                City   State   Zip Code

Address _____
                Number   Street

                 _____
                City   State   Zip Code

ADDRESS _____
                Number   Street

                 _____
                City   State   Zip Code

Address _____
                Number   Street

                 _____
                City   State   Zip Code

LESSON 10 Address—City, State, and Zip Code

It's Your Cue

I live in the city of _____.

I live in the state of _____.

My zip code is _____.

WORD SEARCH 2

Can you find and circle these words?

name	middle	state	telephone
last	address	zip code	social security number
first	city		

---

h	b	s	o	c	i	a	l	d	y	r
b	c	e	f	i	r	s	t	a	x	q
e	f	c	g	t	s	t	l	p	b	o
l	a	u	u	y	v	e	w	r	b	n
g	m	r	p	t	l	z	k	j	c	f
p	z	i	o	d	f	i	n	c	o	j
d	r	t	e	l	e	p	h	o	n	e
o	s	y	q	n	u	v	z	d	r	r
a	d	m	b	n	u	m	b	e	r	j
e	l	k	m	b	a	c	x	g	i	t
n	v	w	x	u	f	b	d	l	m	d
a	d	d	r	e	s	s	i	f	v	h
m	r	d	l	a	s	t	b	c	t	o
e	a	c	k	v	u	a	w	y	c	l
d	o	p	h	k	l	t	s	c	v	n
y	m	i	d	d	l	e	f	x	z	w

CHECKUP 2

NAME _____
          First   MI   Last

ADDRESS _____
            Number   Street

          _____
          City   State   Zip Code

(_____) _____
          Telephone Number

SOCIAL SECURITY NUMBER ☐☐☐ - ☐☐ - ☐☐☐☐

LESSON 11 Marital Status

LESSON 11 Marital Status

Circle the word that is the same.

| Single | Shingle | Signal | Simple | (Single) |

Single	Shingle	Signal	Simple	Single
Married	Marriage	Marred	Married	Market
Separated	September	Separated	Serrated	Served
Divorced	Diverted	Divided	Diverse	Divorced
Widowed	Widowhood	Widower	Widowed	Window

Match the words.

Single   MARRIED

DIVORCED   Widowed

Separated   SINGLE

Married   Divorced

WIDOWED   SEPARATED

LESSON 11 Marital Status 141

LESSON 11 Marital Status

Check.

Single ☐   Single _____

Married ☐   Married _____

Separated ☐   Separated _____

Divorced ☐   Divorced _____

Widowed ☐   Widowed _____

Circle.   Circle.

Single   Single

Married   Married

Separated   Separated

Divorced   Divorced

Widowed   Widowed

LESSON 11 Marital Status

Copy.

Marital Status _____

MARITAL STATUS _____

MARITAL STATUS _____

Marital Status _____

Marital Status _____

MARITAL STATUS _____

Marital Status _____

MARITAL STATUS _____

Marital Status _____

MARITAL STATUS _____

It's Your Cue

I am _____.

LESSON 12 Sex

144

Male   Female

LESSON 12 Sex

Circle the word that is the same.

| Sex | Six | Set | Sew | (Sex) |

Sex	Six	Set	Sew	Sex
Male	Mate	Mile	Male	Make
Female	Finale	Female	Fennel	Film

Match the words.

Sex   Male

Female   Sex

MALE   FEMALE

LESSON 12 Sex

Circle.

Sex: Male   Sex: Male

       Female   Female

Check.

Sex: Male _____   Sex: Male _____

       Female _____   Female _____

Circle.

Sex: M   F   Sex: M   F

Sex: M   F   Sex: M   F

Sex: M   F   Sex: M   F

Sex: M   F   Sex: M   F

Sex: M   F   Sex: M   F

Copy.

Sex _____   Sex _____

Sex _____   Sex _____

Sex _____   Sex _____

Sex _____   Sex _____

LESSON 13 Formal Titles   **147**

LESSON 13 Formal Titles

Match the titles.

Mr.　　　　　　　　　　　　　　　　　　　　　Miss

Miss　　　　　　　　　　　　　　　　　　　　　Mrs.

Mrs.　　　　　　　　　　　　　　　　　　　　　Ms.

Ms.　　　　　　　　　　　　　　　　　　　　　　Mr.

Check.	Circle.	Circle.
Mr. ☐	Mr.	Mr.
Mrs. ☐	Mrs.	Mrs.
Ms. ☐	Ms.	Ms.
Miss ☐	Miss	Miss

It's Your Cue

Mr.

Mrs. _____
　　　　　　Last Name　　　　　　First Name　　　　　MI

Ms.

Miss

CHECKUP 3

Mr.
Mrs. Name _____
Ms.   Last   First   Middle
Miss

Address _____
            Number   Street

          _____
            City   State   Zip Code

Telephone Number _____

Social Security Number _____

Marital Status   **Sex** _____

   Single   _____

   Married   _____

   Separated   _____

   Divorced   _____

   Widowed   _____

WORD SEARCH 3

Can you find and circle these words?

single	separated	male
divorced	widowed	female
married		

n m a r r i e d f g
r a c o u s b i j x
t l q z e s m v w r
f e m a l e c o h d
u y k b c p a r f m
s l n e x a n c k n
l g v g c r e e b l
n f a r g a b d m t
g e w q p t i x n y
l o y t d e d o g p
e u v w i d o w e d

LESSON 14 Height and Weight

LESSON 14 Height and Weight

HEIGHT

inch = in. = "

foot = ft. = '

12 inches = 1 foot

Copy.

STUDENT	INCHES	FEET	INCHES
_____	_____ in.	_____ ft.	_____ in.
_____	_____ in.	_____ ft.	_____ in.
_____	_____ in.	_____ ft.	_____ in.
_____	_____ in.	_____ ft.	_____ in.
_____	_____ in.	_____ ft.	_____ in.
_____	_____ in.	_____ ft.	_____ in.
_____	_____ in.	_____ ft.	_____ in.
_____	_____ in.	_____ ft.	_____ in.

LESSON 14 Height and Weight

Write your height.

HEIGHT _____ ft. _____ in.

Height _____ ft. _____ in.

Height _____ ft. _____ in.

HEIGHT _____ ft. _____ in.

Height _____

HEIGHT _____

HEIGHT _____

Height _____

Height _____

Height _____

HEIGHT _____

HEIGHT _____

LESSON 14 Height and Weight

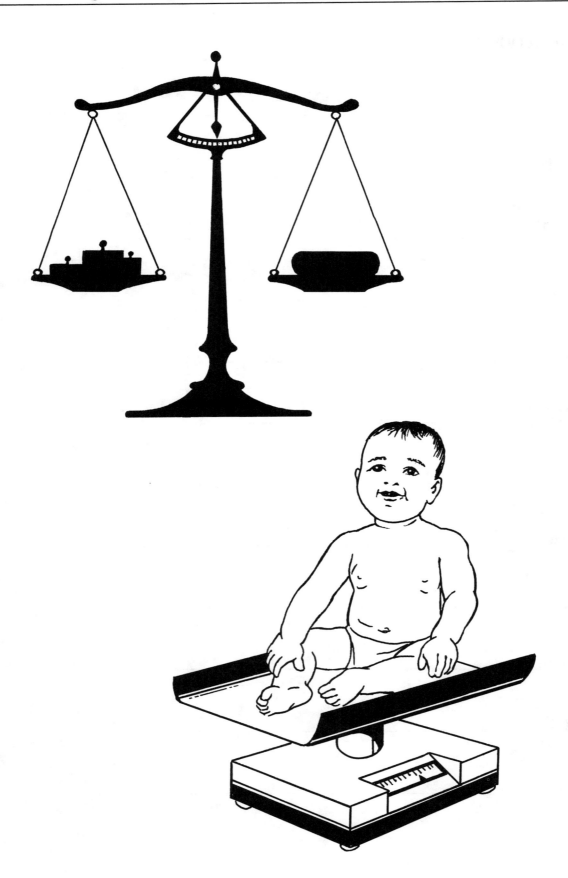

LESSON 14 Height and Weight

WEIGHT

.45 kilograms = 1 pound

ounce = oz.

pound = lb.

16 oz. = 1 lb.

Copy your weight.

WEIGHT _____ lbs.

Weight _____ lbs.

Weight _____ lbs.

WEIGHT _____ lbs.

WEIGHT _____ lbs.

Weight _____ lbs.

Weight _____ lbs.

WEIGHT _____ lbs.

LESSON 14 Height and Weight

Write.

HEIGHT _____ ft. _____ in.

Weight _____ lbs.

WEIGHT _____

Height _____

_____   _____
Height   Weight

_____   _____
WEIGHT   HEIGHT

_____
     Height   Weight

Height _____

Weight _____

It's Your Cue

My height is _____.

My weight is _____.

LESSON 15 Color of Hair and Eyes

LESSON 15 Color of Hair and Eyes

Circle the word that is the same.

brown	blown	blonde	brawn	brown
black	block	brock	black	break
red	led	red	rod	rad
blonde	brown	bland	blonde	brand
green	green	greed	great	grease
blue	blow	blew	boo	blue
gray	grey	gray	gravy	grape
white	white	whirl	wide	whine

Match the words.

brown	black
green	blonde
blonde	brown
blue	green
black	blue
gray	white
white	gray

LESSON 15 Color of Hair and Eyes

Color of eyes   Color of hair

brown   blonde   white
green   red   gray
blue   brown
               black

Copy.

Color of eyes _____

Color of eyes _____

Color of eyes _____

Color of eyes _____

Color of eyes _____

Color of eyes _____

Color of hair _____

Color of hair _____

Color of hair _____

Color of hair _____

Color of hair _____

Color of hair _____

LESSON 15 Color of Hair and Eyes

Write.

Color of eyes _____

Color of hair _____

COLOR OF HAIR _____

Color of Eyes _____

COLOR OF EYES _____

_____   _____
Color of eyes   Color of hair

_____   _____
Color of hair   Color of eyes

_____   _____
COLOR OF EYES   COLOR OF HAIR

Color of hair _____   Color of eyes _____

It's Your Cue

My hair is _____.

My eyes are _____.

WORD SEARCH 4

Can you find and circle these words?

color	green	black	white
hair	brown	blonde	blue
eyes	red	gray	

q b c d o p x y z a
x r o u d t y b w x
t o b d z k q l l j
c w h i t e p o x y
o n f r u y i n t k
l b m c g e n d s o
o j o x b s r e d d
r e t b l u e t n b
f x g r a y p a j n
d e r u c o r t o g
x l e w k y h a i r
y b e n a r l l n x
a v n t s r e t c o

LESSON 16 Place of Birth

Circle the word that is the same.

| PLACE | PAGE | PLACET | (PLACE) | PLAQUE |

PLACE	PACE	PLACET	PLACE	PLAQUE
Of	Or	Off	If	Of
Birth	Birch	Birth	Bird	Berth
Country	County	Court	Courtesy	Country
ORIGIN	ORIGIN	ORIGAN	ORIGINAL	ORGAN

Match the words.

COUNTRY   ORIGIN

OF   PLACE

Origin   BIRTH

Birth   Country

Place   Of

LESSON 16 Place of Birth

Copy.

Place of Birth _____

Place of Birth _____

Place of Birth _____

Place of Birth _____

Country of Origin _____

Country of Origin _____

Country of Origin _____

Country of Origin _____

_____
PLACE OF BIRTH

_____
PLACE OF BIRTH

_____
Country of Origin

_____
COUNTRY OF ORIGIN

LESSON 16 Place of Birth

Write.

_____
Place of Birth

_____
Country of Origin

_____
PLACE OF BIRTH

_____
COUNTRY OF ORIGIN

Place of Birth _____

COUNTRY OF ORIGIN _____

Country of Origin _____

PLACE OF BIRTH _____

_____
PLACE OF BIRTH

_____
COUNTRY OF ORIGIN

It's Your Cue

My place of birth is_____.

LESSON 17 Age

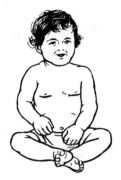

LESSON 17 Age

Write.

Age _____

AGE _____

Age _____

AGE _____

AGE _____

_____
Age

_____
AGE

_____
Age

_____
Age

_____
AGE

Check.

Age

18 - 24 ☐

25 - 30 ☐

31 - 39 ☐

40 - 49 ☐

50 - 65 ☐

66 - 80 ☐

It's Your Cue

I am _____ years old.

LESSON 18 Date

Circle the word that is the same.

| Date | Dot | Dare | (Date) | Dote |

Date	Dot	Dare	Date	Dote
Month	Ninth	Munch	Mount	Month
Day	Date	Day	Bay	Dog
Year	Year	Yeast	Yearn	Yarn

Match the words.

YEAR   Date

Day   MONTH

DATE   Year

Month   DAY

LESSON 18 Date

1. January

2. February

3. March

4. April

5. May

6. June

7. July

8. August

9. September

10. October

11. November

12. December

LESSON 18 Date

169

Copy.

1 January

January

2 February

February

3 March

March

4 April

April

LESSON 18 Date

5   May

May

6   June

June

7   July

July

8   August

August

LESSON 18 Date

9 September

September

10 October

October

11 November

November

12 December

December

LESSON 18 Date

Match the number with the month.

3	August
10	December
7	April
2	June
12	March
9	November
1	October
4	May
8	July
11	January
5	September
6	February

LESSON 18 Date

Write the missing letter.

6   J ___ n e

8   A u ___ u s t

2   F e b ___ u a r y

12   ___ e c e m b e r

4   A p r i ___

9   S e ___ t e m b e r

3   M a r c ___

11   N o ___ e m b e r

5   M a ___

10   O ___ t o b e r

7   J u ___ y

1   J a n ___ a r y

LESSON 18 Date

174

July 27, 1988
↓ ↓ ↓
(Month) (Day) (Year)

January 28, 1989
↓ ↓ ↓
(Month) (Day) (Year)

December 31, 1960
↓ ↓ ↓
(Month) (Day) (Year)

LESSON 18 Date

Circle the date that is the same.

June 1989

				1	2	3
4	5	6	7	8	9	10
11	12	13	14	15	16	17
18	19	20	21	22	(23)	24
25	26	27	28	29	30	

June 22, 1989

June 23, 1988

June 23, 1989

June 30, 1989

October 1989

1	2	3	4	5	6	7
8	9	10	11	12	13	14
15	16	17	18	19	20	21
22	23	24	25	26	27	28
29	30	(31)				

October 13, 1988

October 30, 1938

October 31, 1938

October 31, 1989

LESSON 18 Date

Circle the date that is the same.

January 1990

	1	2	3	4	5	6
7	8	9	10	11	12	13
14	15	16	17	18	19	20
21	22	23	24	25	(26)	27
28	29	30	31			

January 26, 1980

January 25, 1990

January 19, 1990

January 26, 1990

June 1990

					1	2
3	4	5	6	(7)	8	9
10	11	12	13	14	15	16
17	18	19	20	21	22	23
24	25	26	27	28	29	30

June 7, 1999

June 7, 1990

June 7, 1990

June 7, 1980

LESSON 18 Date

Circle the date that is the same.

March 1989

			1	2	3	4
5	6	7	⑧	9	10	11
12	13	14	15	16	17	18
19	20	21	22	23	24	25
26	27	28	29	30	31	

March 3, 1986

March 8, 1989

March 8, 1987

March 9, 1989

February 1990

				1	2	3
4	5	6	7	8	9	10
11	12	13	14	15	16	17
18	19	20	21	22	23	24
25	26	27	㉘			

February 28, 1989

February 23, 1990

February 28, 1990

February 20, 1990

LESSON 18 Date

Complete the calendars.

September 1989

					1	2
3	4	5			8	
10	11	12			15	
17	18		20			23
	25		27		29	

November 1989

				2		4
5			8		10	
		14		16		
19		21				25
26		28		30		

LESSON 18 Date

Complete the calendars.

August 1989

		1	2			
6		8	9			
13			16			
20	21			24		
27				31		

November 1990

				1		
4	5		7	8	9	
	12			15		17
18				22	23	
25			28		30	

LESSON 18 Date _____

Fill in the calendar for this month.

LESSON 18 Date

181

Date of Birth　=　Birth Date

Copy.

DATE OF BIRTH _____

Date of Birth _____

Date of Birth _____

DATE OF BIRTH _____

BIRTH DATE _____

Birth Date _____

BIRTH DATE _____

Birth Date _____

Date of Arrival _____

DATE OF ARRIVAL _____

Date of Arrival _____

DATE OF ARRIVAL _____

LESSON 18 Date

Write.

_____
Date of Birth

_____
DATE OF BIRTH

_____
BIRTH DATE

_____
Date of Arrival

_____
Birth Date

_____
DATE OF ARRIVAL

_____
Date of Birth

_____
Date of Arrival

_____
Birth Date

LESSON 18 Date

Circle the date that is the same.

December 1989

					1	2
3	4	5	6	7	8	9
10	11	⑫	13	14	15	16
17	18	19	20	21	22	23
24	25	26	27	28	29	30
31						

Date: December 12, 1989

    12   12 89

12-12-89

12/12/89

LESSON 18 Date

Circle the date that is the same.

November 1989

		1	2	3	4	5
6	7	8	9	10	11	12
13	14	15	16	17	18	19
20	21	22	23	24	25	26
27	28	29	30			

Date: November 18, 1989

    11   18 89

11-18-89

11/18/89

LESSON 18 Date

Circle the date that is the same.

July 1990

1	2	3	4	5	6	7
8	9	10	11	12	13	14
15	16	17	18	19	20	21
22	23	24	25	26	27	28
29	30	31				

Date: July 5, 1990

7   5   90

7-5-90

7/5/90

LESSON 18 Date

186

Write the missing numbers.

June 16, 1988

    6 /   16   /88
    ―――――――――――――

November 12, 1989

    11 /   /89
    ―――――――――――――

March 5, 1972

       /   5   /72
    ―――――――――――――

December 31, 1965

    12 /   /65
    ―――――――――――――

April 20, 1977

       /   /77
    ―――――――――――――

January 1, 1960

       /   1   /
    ―――――――――――――

May 11, 1980

       /   /
    ―――――――――――――

July 4, 1976

       /   /
    ―――――――――――――

February 15, 1988

       /   /
    ―――――――――――――

August 28, 1977

       /   /
    ―――――――――――――

LESSON 18 Date

Write the missing numbers.

October 7, 1978

_____

February 20, 1970

_____

July 27, 1983

_____

August 8, 1988

_____

September 5, 1989

_____

LESSON 18 Date

Write the dates.

Birth Date		
Month	Day	Year

DATE OF ARRIVAL		
Month	Day	Year

DATE OF BIRTH		
Month	Day	Year

Date of Arrival		
Month	Day	Year

Birth Date		
Month	Day	Year

DATE OF ARRIVAL		
Month	Day	Year

Date of Birth		
Month	Day	Year

Date of Arrival		
Month	Day	Year

LESSON 18 Date

Write today's date.

___/___/___
Date

___/___/___
Date

___/___/___
Date

___-___-___
Date

___-___-___
Date

Date _____
      Month Day Year

Date _____
      Month Day Year

It's Your Cue

My date of birth is _____.

My date of arrival is _____.

Today's date is _____.

CHECKUP 4

Date _____

NAME Mr.
      Ms.
      Mrs. _____
      Miss   First   Middle   Last

ADDRESS _____
            Number   Street

        _____
            City   State   Zip Code

TELEPHONE NUMBER _____
                    Area Code

SOCIAL SECURITY NUMBER ☐☐☐-☐☐-☐☐☐☐

MARITAL STATUS   Single   ☐   SEX M ☐   AGE 18 - 25 ☐

                 Married   ☐   F ☐   26 - 34 ☐

                 Separated ☐   35 - 44 ☐

                 Divorced ☐   45 - 55 ☐

                 Widowed   ☐   56 - 64 ☐

                                                        65 - 80 ☐

DATE OF BIRTH _____
                 Month   Day   Year

CHECKUP 5

SOCIAL SECURITY NUMBER _____ NAME _____ _____ _____
                                                                                                      LAST   FIRST   MI

ADDRESS _____ _____
        Number   Street

_____ _____
City   State   Zip Code

TELEPHONE NUMBER (___) _____

SEX _____ MARITAL STATUS _____ AGE _____

BIRTH DATE _____ PLACE OF BIRTH _____

Copyright © 1990 Claudia J. Rucinski

CHECKUP 6

Date _____

Name Mr.
      Ms.
      Mrs. _____
      Miss   Last   First   Middle

Address _____
        Number   Street

        _____
        City   State   Zip Code

Telephone Number (___) _____

Social Security Number ☐☐☐ – ☐☐ – ☐☐☐☐

Sex: M   F   Marital Status: Single   _____
                                        Married   _____
                                        Separated _____
                                        Divorced _____
                                        Widowed   _____

Place of Birth _____

Age _____   Height _____   Weight _____

Color of hair _____

Color of eyes _____

CHECKUP 7

Date _____

Name _____ Social Security Number _____

Address _____ _____
(NUMBER) (STREET)

_____ _____ _____
(City) (State) (Zip Code)

Telephone _____ Date of Birth _____

___ Male   ___ Single   Height _____ ft. _____ in.
___ Female ___ Married   Weight _____ lbs.
           ___ Separated   Color of hair _____
           ___ Divorced   Color of eyes _____
           ___ Widowed

Place of Birth _____ Date of Arrival _____

CHECKUP 8

	Month	Day	Year
Social Security Number			

Last Name	First Name	MI

Address	Number	Street

City	State	Zip Code

Area Code	Telephone

Sex	Marital Status

	Month	Day	Year
Date of Birth			

	Month	Day	Year
Date of Arrival			

Height	Weight

Color of Hair	Color of Eyes

Country of Origin

STUDENT PROGRESS CHART FOR: _____

Handout	Date Completed	Checked By	Comments
1			
2			
3			
4			
5			
6			
7			
8			
9			
10			
11			
12			
13			
14			
15			
16			
17			
18			
19			
20			
21			
22			
23			
24			
25			

STUDENT PROGRESS CHART FOR: _____

Handout	Date Completed	Checked By	Comments
26			
27			
28			
29			
30			
31			
32			
33			
34			
35			
36			
37			
38			
39			
40			
41			
42			
43			
44			
45			
46			
47			
48			
49			
50			

STUDENT PROGRESS CHART FOR:

Handout	Date Completed	Checked By	Comments
51			
52			
53			
54			
55			
56			
57			
58			
59			
60			
61			
62			
63			
64			
65			
66			
67			
68			
69			
70			
71			
72			
73			
74			
75			

STUDENT PROGRESS CHART FOR:

Handout	Date Completed	Checked By	Comments
76			
77			
78			
79			
80			
81			
82			
83			
84			
85			
86			
87			
88			
89			
90			
91			
92			
93			
94			
95			
96			
97			
98			
99			
100			

STUDENT PROGRESS CHART FOR:

Handout	Date Completed	Checked By	Comments
101			
102			
103			
104			
105			
106			
107			
108			
109			
110			
111			
112			
113			
114			
115			
116			
117			
118			
119			
120			
121			
122			
123			
124			
125			

STUDENT PROGRESS CHART FOR: _____

Handout	Date Completed	Checked By	Comments
126			
127			
128			
129			
130			
131			
132			
133			
134			
135			
136			
137			
138			
139			
140			
141			
142			
143			
144			
145			
146			
147			
148			
149			
150			

Copyright © 1990 Claudia J. Rucinski

STUDENT PROGRESS CHART FOR: _____

Handout	Date Completed	Checked By	Comments
151			
152			
153			
154			
155			
156			
157			
158			
159			
160			
161			
162			
163			
164			
165			
166			
167			
168			
169			
170			
171			
172			
173			
174			
175			

STUDENT PROGRESS CHART FOR: _____

Handout	Date Completed	Checked By	Comments
176			
177			
178			
179			
180			
181			
182			
183			
184			
185			
186			
187			
188			
189			
190			
191			
192			
193			
194			